Wine Country Bike Rides

Wine Country Bike Rides

THE BEST TOURS IN SONOMA, NAPA, AND MENDOCINO COUNTIES

BY LENA EMMERY

CHRONICLE BOOKS
SAN FRANCISCO

Printed in the United States of America.

Library of Congress Cataloging-in-Publication Data:

Emmery, Lena.
    Wine country bike rides: the best tours in Sonoma, Napa, and Mendocino
Counties / by Lena Emmery ; [maps, Bob Aufuldish & Stella Lai]
            p.   cm.
    Includes index.
    ISBN 0-8118-1355-X (pbk.)
    1. Bicycle touring—California—Sonoma County—Guidebooks.
2. Bicycle touring—California—Napa County—Guidebooks.
3. Bicycle touring—California—Mendocino County—Guidebooks.
4. Sonoma County (Calif.)—Guidebooks. 5. Napa County (Calif.)—Guidebooks.
6.Mendocino County (Calif.)—Guidebooks.   I.Title
GV1045.5C22S664   1997
796.6'4'097941—dc20   96-32452
                                                                      CIP

Cover Photograph: Sterling Vineyards by
Roger Paperno
Cover and book design
Aufuldish & Warinner
Maps by
Bob Aufuldish & Stella Lai

Distributed in Canada by Raincoast Books
9050 Shaughnessy Street, Vancouver, B.C. V6p 6E5

10 9 8 7 6 5 4 3 2

Chronicle Books LLC
85 Second Street
San Francisco, CA 94105

www.chroniclebooks.com

DEDICATED TO SALLY TAYLOR

A WORLD CLASS CYCLIST AND FRIEND WITHOUT WHOSE
GENEROUS SUPPORT AND
ENCOURAGEMENT THIS BOOK WOULD NOT
HAVE BEEN POSSIBLE.

CONTENTS

8   INTRODUCTION

13   SAN FRANCISCO TO MARIN

15   ❶ Across the Golden Gate Bridge

20   SONOMA COUNTY

21   Key Map A

22   SONOMA VALLEY

25   ❷ Sonoma Town Ride

27   ❸ Valley of the Moon

31   ❹ Glen Ellen Loop

33   RUSSIAN RIVER AREA

37   ❺ Forestville Summer Loop

39   ❻ Russian River

43   ❼ Eastside, Westside

45   ❽ Dry Creek

49   ❾ Alexander Valley

53   ❿ Geyserville Loop

55 **MENDOCINO COUNTY**

56 EASTERN MENDOCINO COUNTY

57 ⓫ Hopland Area

61 ⓬ Rambling Round Ukiah

63 ⓭ Redwood Valley

66 ANDERSON VALLEY

69 ⓮ North to Navarro

72 ⓯ Philo to Boonville

74 **NAPA COUNTY**

75 Key Map B

76 NORTHERN NAPA VALLEY

79 ⓰ Calistoga

85 ⓱ St. Helena

89 ⓲ St. Helena to Rutherford

92 SOUTHERN NAPA VALLEY

93 ⓳ Yountville, Stags Leap District

99 ⓴ The Carneros District

102 INDEX OF WINERIES AND

STOPPING SITES

Introduction

**ELCOME TO THE WORLD OF VINEYARDS** *seen at close range, where the bicycle adds a wonderful dimension to the trip. The microclimates so often referred to by vintners are, somehow, much more compelling after one has personally ridden through them, pedaling up and down the hills and feeling the wind at one's back. The textures and aromas of the land that are so much a part of viticulture are naturally incorporated into a bicycle trip. Getting there is truly half the fun when you choose a bicycle as a vehicle. Come along and enjoy the ride.*

We start in San Francisco and cover Napa, Sonoma, and Mendocino counties, three of the four counties in the North Coast wine country. By way of introduction I have also included an especially scenic tour to a Marin County tasting room.

Many of the wineries I have included are small. Call ahead if you must visit a particular winery; sometimes they just take a day off! All the wineries are closed on major holidays such as Christmas and New Year's Day.

I have included a limited selection of places to stay, ranging from campgrounds to bed-and-breakfast inns. The places to visit that are mentioned are only a small sample of what is available in the wine country. You will find many more surprises to enjoy.

This book assumes that you have some experience riding a bicycle, although you need not be an expert to enjoy these trips. You need to have a working knowledge of your bicycle so that minor repairs and flat tires (the most common ailment) can be easily tended to on the road. Read the section on preparing your bicycle prior to your trip (pages 10–11). The law requires that helmets be worn by all minors. Good sense indicates that anyone on a bicycle should wear a helmet. Even the Tour de France riders are sporting them these days. The latest generation of helmets are light, relatively inexpensive, and well designed. Look for the Snell approval on the helmet.

The maps show the routes clearly. In addition I recommend that you carry the text with you so you stay found. The mileages given are approximate and are based on Avocet odometer readings. They include road distances but exclude the driveways from the entry gates to the winery buildings.

In the warm months from May through September, I urge you to ride early and avoid the heat of the day. Always carry plenty of water or special drinks to replace lost electrolytes.

This book recognizes that while you are riding through the wine country, you may desire to sample the wines. I cannot recommend this practice except in moderation since, on a bicycle, everyone is the designated driver. The vehicle code gives bicycle riders the same rights and responsibilities as automobile drivers. The limits on blood alcohol apply to cyclists just as they do to drivers. Know your limits and understand the risk you are taking if you drink and ride.

PREPARING YOUR BICYCLE

If you do not own a bicycle, you can rent one easily. Make sure the bicycle fits you in size and purpose. I mention some places to rent bicycles at the start of each section of this book.

If you do own a bicycle but it does not get ridden on a regular basis, have it checked by a reputable bicycle shop before your trip. Be sure that all rubber parts such as brake shoes and tires are checked carefully, since they deteriorate with age. All the cables for brakes and derrailleurs should also be checked for replacement as needed. In addition, you may want to have the gear ratios adjusted for more range.

While you're at the bike shop, pick up some basic tools and a pouch to carry them in. Your kit should include the following items.

TO REPAIR A FLAT TIRE:

• Tire pump that fits the valves on your tires. There are two common kinds, Shrader and Presta.

• Spare inner tube, or two; check for correct size and valve type.

• Patch kit, in case you ruin your spare tube. Glue is available in tiny tubes so it does not dry out. Glue-less patches are an alternate, but these get mixed reviews.

• Tire levers, usually three to a set.

FOR GENERAL REPAIRS:

• Multipurpose tool, screwdriver, wrench, etc., suitable for the bolts and nuts on your bicycle.

• Small rag and moist towel to clean up after repair.

PERSONAL ITEMS:

• Small first-aid kit.

• Water bottle and holder to attach to the bicycle frame.

• Windbreaker or rain jacket, depending on the skies.

SECURITY ITEMS:

• Good quality lock if you plan to leave your bicycle for even a few minutes.

• Cash and a credit card for when all else fails.

I highly recommend that your bicycle be equipped with a bell to signal your presence. Riding at dusk or in the dark is discouraged, but you should still carry bicycle lights for the front and rear in case circumstances delay your return. The law also requires an assortment of reflectors, which your local bike shop should have available.

PREPARING YOUR BODY

This one is up to you and, perhaps, your physician. Check with your doctor if you have any doubts about your physical condition.

If you are not a regular rider, a few short rides will help your body adjust to bicycle riding. Even a half hour each day will be useful. Practice using the gears to develop a good, steady cycling style. The right equipment is worth the expenditure. A bicycle that has been correctly fitted to you will make a world of difference. Bicycle shorts are more than a fashion statement! They really help cushion your body from the saddle. Rigid shoes are also important for efficiency and good foot protection.

Most of the rides in this book are short enough so that average riders should be able to enjoy themselves. Where major hills are included, they are an option for the experienced rider who is looking for a challenge. Remember, if you're not having fun, you've missed the point!

San Francisco to Marin

Across the Golden Gate Bridge

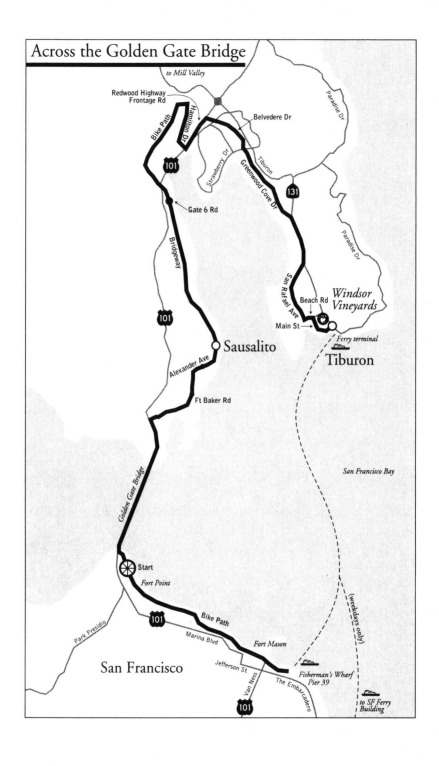

to Mill Valley

Redwood Highway
Frontage Rd

Bike Path

Hamilton Dr

Belvedere Dr

101

Paradise Dr

Strawberry Dr

Greenwood Cove Dr

Tiburon

131

Gate 6 Rd

Paradise Dr

Bridgeway

101

San Rafael Ave

Windsor
Vineyards

Beach Rd

Main St

Ferry terminal

Sausalito

Tiburon

Alexander Ave

Ft Baker Rd

San Francisco Bay

Golden Gate Bridge

Start

Fort Point

(weekdays only)

101

Bike Path

Park Presidio

Marina Blvd

Fort Mason

San Francisco

Jefferson St

Van Ness

The Embarcadero

Fisherman's Wharf
Pier 39

to SF Ferry
Building

101

❶ Across the Golden Gate Bridge

Fabulous views, a ferryboat ride, and some wine tasting.

Approximately 19 miles.

STARTING THE RIDE *Start this ride at the San Francisco end of the Golden Gate Bridge, in the east parking area. You're likely to see other cyclists gathered here. Parking is metered, but if you drive to the start, free parking is available west of the bridge. Take the tunnel under the bridge and park in the unpaved area a short distance up the hill.*

If you have never ridden more than a few miles, this ride is designed to give you a feel for the skills involved without taking you too far from San Francisco. This is also a great ride for tourists, since it is uniquely beautiful and involves great sightseeing opportunities. In the whole world of bike rides, I'd say this is one in a million. Be sure to bring a good lock if you plan to be out of sight of your bicycle.

You can ride across the bridge every day of the week, twenty-four hours a day, thanks to the efforts of local cyclists. In 1970 Elizabeth Terwilliger, a Bay Area conservationist, led the first legal ride across the bridge. Prior to that date, you had to walk past the first tower, then stealthily mount your bike and hope that the police would leave you alone. We've come a long way since then. The weekend, holiday, and late-afternoon route is on the Pacific side of the bridge, on the west walkway. The weekday route is on the bay side of the bridge on the east walkway. Always be considerate; this is an active bicycle corridor. Be sure to have a bell to alert others of your approach.

Golden Gate Transit, which runs bus service between Marin County and San Francisco, has a limited bicycle policy, so if you really get stuck you can ride on bus routes 80, 70, and 60 and get back to San Francisco. The stops for these routes are adjacent to Highway 101. Basic hours are non-commute times, with a two-bike limit per bus. You will be bumped if a handicapped person needs the space.

PLACES TO STAY

San Francisco has a myriad of places to stay, too many to include here. These two hostels offer affordable lodging close to the ride.

American Youth Hostels:

Fort Mason, San Francisco. (415) 771-7277.

Fort Barry, Sausalito. (415) 331-2777.

BICYCLE ASSISTANCE

SAN FRANCISCO:

Marina Cyclery, 3330 Steiner Street, San Francisco. (415) 929-7135.
Monday–Saturday, 10:00–6:00; Sunday, 10:00–5:00.
Rentals available.

Velo City Cyclery, 638 Stanyan Street, San Francisco. (415) 221-2453.
Friday–Monday, 10:00–6:00; Wednesday, 2:00–7:00; Thursday by
appointment; closed Tuesday. Rentals available.

SAUSALITO:

Bicycle Odyssey, 1417 Bridgeway, Sausalito. (415) 332-3050.
Monday–Saturday, 10:00–7:00; Sunday, 10:00–5:00.

Sausalito Cyclery, 1 Gate Six Road, Sausalito. (415) 332-3200.
Monday–Saturday, 10:00–6:00; Sunday, 11:00–5:00.

TRANSPORTATION INFORMATION

Golden Gate Bridge Toll Plaza Administrative Offices. (415) 921-5858.

Golden Gate Transit, for bike/bus information. (415) 923-2000.

Tiburon Ferry, Main Street and Paradise Drive, Tiburon.
(800) 229-2784 for complete timetable and fare information.

THIS RIDE IS MUCH MORE DIFFICULT TO DESCRIBE THAN IT IS TO ACTUALLY TRAVEL! YOUR EFFORTS WILL BE RICHLY REWARDED.

On weekends: From the metered parking area, ride up the short hill to
the bridge. A sign will guide you to the right and along the path that
winds under the bridge to the west side of the structure. Continue
north on the bridge sidewalk, taking extra care around the towers
because the wind can be unpredictable. The ride across the bridge is
about 1¹/₂ miles. A few feet after the north tower, turn left onto the
concrete bicycle bridge. Head downhill with a right turn and follow this
road under the bridge and along the water through Fort Baker. After a

short uphill, the road joins Alexander Avenue.

On weekdays: Stay on the east sidewalk. You will be sharing the route with pedestrians and bridge maintenance crews, who have the right of way. Once across the bridge, you'll be in a parking area. Ride to the far side of the parking area and continue on the bike path as it parallels the freeway. This will guide you onto Alexander Avenue and the splendid downhill into Sausalito. The shoulder is accommodating, but look out for erratic winds and runners.

After about 3¼ miles, Alexander Avenue becomes Bridgeway and continues downhill into and through Sausalito. There is a bike path shortly after the downtown area, but it is obscure and a bit of an obstacle course—with stairs! The shoulder is generally good and Marin drivers are considerate, so the road is an acceptable choice. Bridgeway ends at the freeway in about 3 miles at the junction of Gate Six Road. This is where you must get on the bike path, which is on your right at water's edge, and sometimes, at very high tides, under water. You'll be cycling through the Bothin Marsh Open Space Preserve. Meander another 2 miles, turn right, and cross the small wooden bridge. The path runs into Hamilton Drive in about ½ mile; when you see a firehouse directly in front of you, turn right.

This section of road is one way except for bicycles. Doesn't that make you feel special? Go up a small hill and then down the other side to the intersection of Redwood Highway Frontage Road, about ½ mile. Turn right and continue on the Frontage Road, bearing left under Highway 101. (You've reversed your direction at this point.) Pedal along the other side of the freeway until you get to Belvedere Drive; it's about a mile. Turn right and cruise for a mile through this pleasant suburban neighborhood. The road ends at Strawberry Drive. Make a left and then an immediate right onto Tiburon Boulevard. In less than ¼ mile, turn right at the intersection of Greenwood Cove Drive.

This quiet road changes its name to Greenwood Beach Road before it ends at Richardson Bay Park in about a mile. Don't let the obstacle course at the end of Greenwood discourage you; it is there to keep automobiles from going through. You'll now be on Brunini Way. The bike path that goes through the park is toward the left. In a mile it intersects San Rafael Avenue; turn right here and continue along the water until the road meets Beach Road. Turn left and make the next right onto Main Street.

Another ¹/2 mile and you'll see the front door to *Windsor Vineyards Tiburon Wine Tasting Room* on your left. Stop here to sample a wide variety of wines from this Sonoma County winery in a peaceful suburban setting. The manager, Ron Skellenger, will give a friendly greeting and invite you to sample wines that have consistently won more awards for high quality than those of any other winery. You can arrange to have your favorite wine shipped to most destinations. When you leave the tasting room, turn left and continue another ¹/2 mile on Main Street to the intersection of Tiburon Boulevard, where signs will direct you to the San Francisco Ferry Terminal.

Plan to linger a while in Tiburon. This charming village has lots of shops, restaurants, and bakeries. Among my favorite attractions are Sweden House and Boudin Bakery Cafe, both of which have great bakery treats and light lunch items. For more substantial fare, try Sam's Anchor Cafe or Guaymas. There will be plenty to keep you content until the ferry arrives to whisk you back to San Francisco.

Bicycles travel free of charge on the ferries; people, however, have to pay. Departures from Tiburon start at approximately 11:40 A.M. on weekends, with the last run from Tiburon at around 6:50 P.M. During the week, departures from Tiburon start at 6:00 A.M. Times vary with the season, so you should verify these times by calling the number listed in the Transportation Information section at the start of this chapter (page 16). There is a limit of twenty-five bicycles on each boat, so don't bring all your friends!

Weekends, the Tiburon Ferry has only one San Francisco destination, Fisherman's Wharf/Pier 39. During the week, an additional option is the Ferry Building.

(During the week, if you arrive at the Ferry Building turn right onto the Embarcadero and ride about 1 mile to Pier 39.)

From Pier 39, continue west on Jefferson Street until it ends, a little past Hyde Street, about 1¹/4 miles. From here you can ride on the multiuse path that is a part of the San Francisco Bay Trail. When you reach a road, in less than ¹/4 mile, turn right for a few hundred feet, then left—uphill—into Fort Mason. Follow the road over this steep hill, where the view will give you a good excuse to walk. Once over the top, it's an easy coast down to Marina Boulevard. Continue on Marina Boulevard, or on the informal bike trail that parallels it, one mile; you'll be in the Presidio on Mason Street. The Presidio of San Francisco is a part of the Golden Gate National Recreation Area. Look left and you can see some of the historical buildings. This area recently became a park after it was no longer in use by the military. The roads may be confusing as a result of this transition.

The Golden Gate Bridge, your destination, will be in clear view. Keep this in mind and you will stay found.

Proceed a mile to the end of Crissy Field and turn right on Livingston Street. At the end of this one-block street turn left. Keep to the right and in $1/4$ mile you'll be on the path that aligns with the water's edge. After the unpaved section of about $1/4$ mile, turn left onto the paved road. If you wish to visit historic Fort Point, make a right turn and ride $1/2$ mile. If the direct route is your choice, turn left and head up the short hill on Long Avenue. At the end of Long Avenue turn right again onto Lincoln Boulevard. Continue on Lincoln $1/2$ mile and turn right into the east parking lot of the Golden Gate Bridge Toll Plaza, where you started.

WINERIES

Windsor Vineyards Tiburon Wine Tasting Room, 72 main Street, Tiburon 94920. (415) 435-1269. Daily, 10:00–6:00.

STOPPING SITES

Fisherman's Wharf. Jefferson Street between Powell and Hyde Streets.

Fort Mason Center. Buchanan and Marina Boulevard.

Fort Point and Presidio Historical Association. (415) 921-8193.

Boudin Bakery Cafe, 1 Main Street, Tiburon. (415) 435-0777. Open daily.

Guaymas Restaurant, 5 Main Street, Tiburon. (415) 435-6300. Open daily.

Sam's Anchor Cafe, 27 Main Street, Tiburon. (415) 435-4527. Open daily.

Sweden House Bakery, 35 Main Street, Tiburon. (415) 435-9767. Open daily.

Sonoma County

SONOMA VALLEY

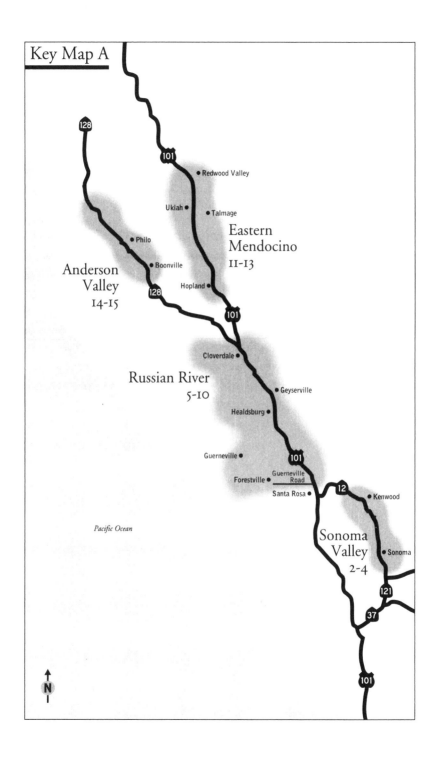

Sonoma Valley

GETTING THERE *The town of Sonoma is about one hour from San Francisco by car. Head north on Highway 101. Take the Sonoma/Napa turnoff and proceed along Highway 37. Turn left at Highway 121, and continue to Highway 12; bear right here and proceed for a few miles. Then follow Highway 12 left, and motor into downtown Sonoma. The roads are all well marked, and Key Map A (page 21) should get you there without trouble.*

SONOMA IS A GREAT PLACE TO BEGIN A LOVE AFFAIR WITH THE WINE REGIONS OF CALIFORNIA. There are three rides here for you to enjoy. Ride 2 is short and sweet, about ten miles; Ride 3 is a bit longer, at about seventeen miles, with one real hill and a small section of Highway 12; Ride 4 is about twenty-one miles and includes some longer hills and a bit of a busy section of Highway 12. Each ride has at least one section that is contiguous with one of the other rides, so you can combine them to create a custom tour to suit your abilities and available time. Consult the website noted in additional information section (next page) for special events that may be taking place during your visit.

PLACES TO STAY

CAMPING

Sugarloaf Ridge State Park, 2 miles NE of Kenwood via Adobe
Canyon Road. (707) 833-5712. Open all year. Fees are up to
$16.00 per night.

BED AND BREAKFAST

Glenelly Inn, 5131 Warm Springs Road, Glen Ellen 95442.
(707) 996-6720. You pass by this lovely inn on Ride 3.

Wine Country Inns of Sonoma County is an agency that represents
various inns. P.O. Box 51, Geyserville 95476. (707) 433-4667.

HOTELS

Sonoma Valley Inn Best Western, 550 2nd St. West, Sonoma 95476.
(707) 938-9200 or (800) 334-5784.

BICYCLE ASSISTANCE

Goodtimes Bicycles, 18503 Highway 12 near Thompson Ave.,
Sonoma 95432. Monday–Saturday, 9:00–6:00; Sunday, 10:00–4:00.
(707) 938-0453. Sales, service, and rentals. 21 years in business.

Sonoma Valley Cyclery, 1061 Broadway, Sonoma 95431.
(707) 935-3377. Monday–Saturday, 10:00–6:00;
Sunday, 10:00–4:00. Sales, service, and rentals.

ADDITIONAL INFORMATION

Grapevine Website will give you current events, http://www.winery.com.

Sonoma Town Ride

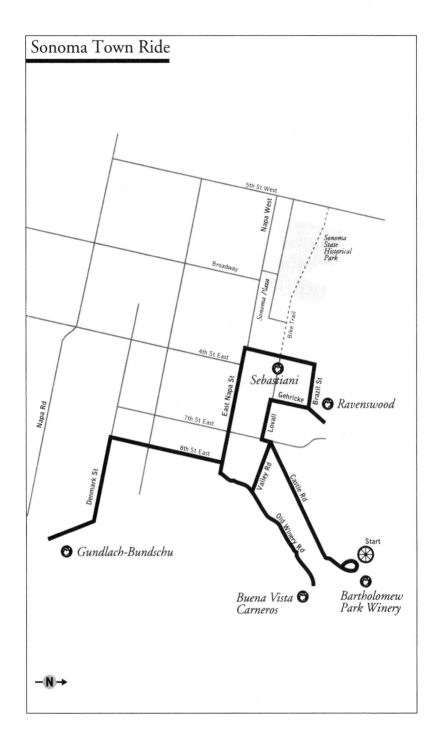

5th St West

Napa West

Sonoma State Historical Park

Broadway

Sonoma Plaza

Bike Trail

4th St East

Sebastiani

East Napa St

Gehricke

Brazil St

Ravenswood

Napa Rd

7th St East

Lovall

8th St East

Denmark St

Valley Rd

Castle Rd

Old Winery Rd

Start

Gundlach-Bundschu

Buena Vista Carneros

Bartholomew Park Winery

N

Sonoma Town Ride

Easy roads and a handful of wineries.

Approximately 10 miles.

STARTING THE RIDE *This is a beautiful ride that provides a good sense of the area and its wines in a very short distance. This ride begins at Bartholomew Park Winery, on Vineyard Lane in Sonoma. There is ample parking for your car there. To get to the winery from Highway 12 Broadway going north, turn right onto East Napa Street and continue to Old Winery Road. Turn left here and continue to Lovall Valley Road. Proceed a mile or so, then make a sharp right onto Castle Road; at the end you will find Vineyard Lane and the start of Ride 2.*

Bartholomew Park Winery is a new winery located in a beautiful park by the same name. The museum there will give you a good overview of the area and its wine-making history. As you leave, be mindful of the speed bumps along the driveway; they are nasty on a bicycle.

After almost 1 mile, you will be at the intersection of Castle and 7th Street East. In a few pedals, turn right onto Lovall Road. In another ¹/₂ mile, turn right at Gehricke Road.

Ravenswood Winery is located ¹/₄ mile up this road, on the pretty hillside at the left. This winery, famous for its hearty Zinfandels, has a loyal following. Return via Gehricke Road and turn right in about ¹/₈ mile at Brazil, a nice country lane. Brazil ends at 4th Street East.

A left turn is the only choice. Continue another ¹/₄ mile to *Sebastiani Vineyards,* at 4th and Lovall. This large winery has a great tour. It also offers a discount on wine to senior citizens. (Here you can add a side trip on the bike path located directly across 4th Street. See Ride 3 (pages 27–29).

After the Sebastiani tour, make a left onto 4th Street heading south, toward town. In a few blocks, turn left onto East Napa Street. (You may want to detour here to the Plaza for picnic supplies such as bread from the famous Sonoma French Bakery and cheese from the Sonoma Cheese Factory. Or stop at the Marketplace Shopping Center for a variety of foods. In that case make a right on West Napa Street and proceed for three blocks.) Another mile brings you to 8th Street; make a right turn and head south about ³/₄ mile until Denmark Road.

Turn left here and proceed about ¹/₂ mile to *Gundlach-Bundschu Winery.* The driveway to the winery is up a long hill, and the road is a little rough and narrow, but the challenge is rewarded by a view as remarkable as the high quality wine produced here. Return to 8th via Denmark and head north, to the right. At East Napa Street take a right; then turn left in about 15 feet onto Old Winery Road.

A small climb leads to *Buena Vista Carneros,* the oldest winery in the North Coast. The old stone building is the perfect site for savoring history and wine. Return down the hill, turn right onto Lovall Valley Road, and proceed about ¹/₂ mile to Castle. Head up the last hill to the starting point and a picnic lunch.

WINERIES

Bartholomew Park Winery, 1000 Vineyard Lane, Sonoma 95476.
(707) 935-9511. Daily, 10:30–4:30.

Buena Vista Carneros, 18000 Old Winery Road, Sonoma 95476.
(707) 938-1266. Daily, 10:30–4:30.

Gundlach-Bundschu Winery, 2000 Denmark Road, Sonoma 95476.
(707) 938-5277. Daily, 11:00–4:30.

Ravenswood Winery, 18701 Gehricke Road, Sonoma 95476.
(707) 938-1960. Daily, 10:30–4:30.

Sebastiani Vineyards, 389 Fourth Street, Sonoma 95476.
(707) 938-5532. Daily, 10:30–5:00.

STOPPING SITES

Marketplace Shopping Center, 201 W. Napa Street, Sonoma.
(707) 935-1366.

Sonoma Cheese Factory, 2 West Spain Street, Sonoma.
(707) 996-1931.

Sonoma French Bakery, 470 1st St. East, Sonoma. (707) 996-2691.

❸ Valley of the Moon

History, hills, and four wineries.

Approximately 17 miles.

STARTING THE RIDE *This easy ride passes through some old history from the Spanish Colonial Era. It includes the Valley of the Moon which was the setting for my favorite of Jack London's writings and where he made his home. Start this ride at Sebastiani Vineyards, 389 Fourth Street East. (See Ride 2, pages 25–26, for directions to Sebastiani.)*

Directly across from the winery, near the intersection of Lovall and 4th, is a bike path which, unlike many such paths, actually goes somewhere. This path provides a nice, relaxed vantage point for viewing the surrounding hills and local park land. Ride through the Sonoma Historic Park and explore one of the local sites of Spanish history. In about 1½ miles the path ends at Highway 12.

Turn right onto Highway 12 with caution, and then at the intersection in one-half block make a left onto Verano Drive. Proceed on for about 1 mile to Arnold Drive. Turn right toward Glen Ellen. Arnold Drive is a busy road, but it has a good shoulder for cycling.

After about 4 miles on Arnold Drive, Jack London Village will be on your right. You may want to stop to visit this tourist attraction. Another ½ mile brings you into the sleepy little town of Glen Ellen, immortalized by Jack London in his writings. If you've already worked up an appetite for lunch, the Glen Ellen Village Market makes extra-large sandwiches and has a nice seating area behind the store.

From Arnold Drive, a left turn onto London Ranch Road starts the significant ½ mile climb to *Benziger Family Winery.* The driveway has speed bumps and a cattle grate; be careful. This winery has a lot for you to explore. It has an outstanding display of viticulture techniques in the Discovery Center, everything from rootstock to trellis systems. Don't forget to check out the wine before you depart. Ride downhill as you leave the winery; at the bottom turn left onto Arnold Drive.

Proceed along Arnold Drive about 1 mile to Highway 12; turn right and move with caution. On your left, ½ mile up the road, is

Valley of the Moon

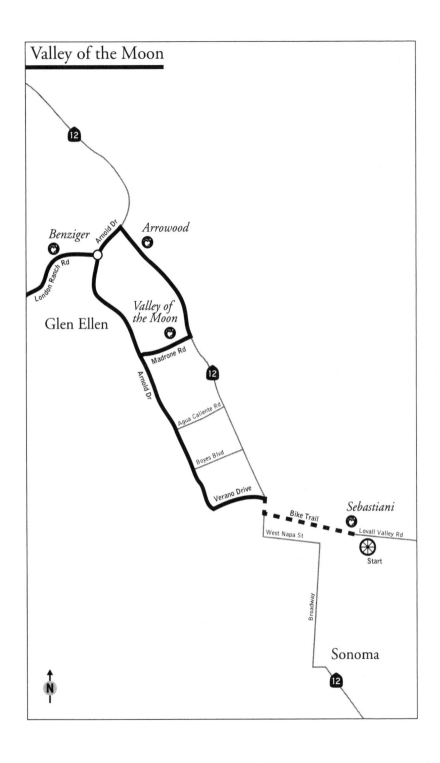

12

Benziger

Arnold Dr

Arrowood

London Ranch Rd

Valley of the Moon

Glen Ellen

Madrone Rd

Arnold Dr

12

Agua Caliente Rd

Boyes Blvd

Verano Drive

Bike Trail

Sebastiani

Lovall Valley Rd

West Napa St

Start

Broadway

Sonoma

12

N

Arrowood Vineyards and Winery. Richard and Alis Arrowood started this winery, an exercise in elegance, in 1987. Richard spent sixteen years at Chateau St. Jean perfecting his wine-making techniques. The focus at Arrowood is on Cabernet Sauvignon, Chardonnay, and Merlot varietals.

Continue on Highway 12 another mile and turn right onto Madrone Road; 1/4 mile on your right will be *Valley of the Moon Winery.* Weekends from early May to the end of September, Southern- style barbecue is available in the vineyard for under $10. Valley of the Moon is one of the few wineries to make a European-style port along with their other products.

Swing back onto Madrone and pedal the 1/2 mile to Arnold Drive, where you should make a left turn and retrace your steps 2 3/4 miles until you reach Verano Drive. Take the bike path, which is a little hard to see from this direction, and ride 1 1/2 miles back to *Sebastiani Vineyards.*

WINERIES

Arrowood Vineyards, 14347 Sonoma Highway, Glen Ellen 95442. (707) 938-5170. Daily, 10:00–4:30.

Benziger Family Winery, 1883 Jack London Ranch Road, Glen Ellen 95442. (707) 935-4076. Daily, 10:00–4:30.

Sebastiani Vineyards, 389 Fourth Street, Sonoma 95476. (707) 938-5532. Daily, 10:30–4:30.

Valley of the Moon Winery, 777 Madrone Road, Glen Ellen 95442. (707) 996-6941. Daily, 10:00–5:00.

STOPPING SITES

Glen Ellen Village Market, 13751 Arnold Drive, Glen Ellen. (707) 996-6728.

Jack London Village, 14301 Arnold Drive, Glen Ellen. (707) 996-5582.

Sonoma State Historic Park, tours with prior reservation. (707) 938-1519.

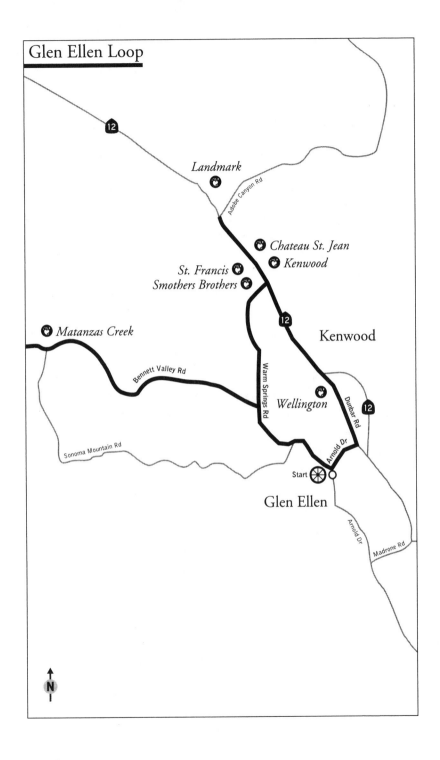

Glen Ellen Loop

Landmark

Adobe Canyon Rd

Chateau St. Jean
Kenwood

St. Francis
Smothers Brothers

Matanzas Creek

Kenwood

Bennett Valley Rd

Warm Springs Rd

Dunbar Rd

Wellington

Sonoma Mountain Rd

Arnold Dr

Start

Glen Ellen

Arnold Dr

Madrone Rd

N

❹ Glen Ellen Loop

Rolling hills, warm springs, and seven wineries.

Approximately 21 miles.

STARTING THE RIDE *Ride 3 (pages 27–29) takes you to Glen Ellen. • This hilly ride, which starts on Arnold Drive in Glen Ellen, is one of my favorites in the early spring, when it is not too hot. Even on a rainy winter day this is a lovely ride. (If you want to do more miles, follow the directions from Sonoma to Glen Ellen in Ride 3.)*

From Arnold Drive, take a left turn onto Warm Springs Road shortly after the small bridge. After 2³/4 miles you will be at the intersection of Bennett Valley Road. Turn left to begin the climb up Bennett Valley Road through some really lovely countryside.

In 5 miles, on the right, the lavender plants at the gate offer a warm welcome to *Matanzas Creek Winery.* This winery produces Bordeaux-style wines with exceptional attention to detail. It also sells lavender products made from its own plantings. Creative sculptures add to the interest.

Return to Bennett Valley Road to enjoy the downhill. When you reach Warm Springs Road, turn left and pedal to the famous Morton's Warm Springs, where you can stop for a dip in their pear-shaped pool. Continue on the 2³/4 miles to Highway 12.

Directly across the road will be *Kenwood Vineyards.* The simple barn that serves as a tasting room belies the quality of the wines. Kenwood prides itself on good, solid, dependable wines.

From there, turn right to neighboring *Chateau St. Jean.* This stylish winery is best known for superb white wines and late-harvest specialties, all carefully made. The grounds invite you to linger.

Turn right from Chateau St. Jean for a short hop to Adobe Canyon Road, the home of *Landmark Vineyards.* It produces only Chardonnays, with grapes coming from three different vineyards, and has a fabulous facility for you to enjoy. With prior reservation, a cottage overlooking the vineyards is available for overnight stays. A new restaurant, The Buckley Lodge, a mile up the road, features gourmet fare.

From Adobe Canyon Road turn left, south, on Highway 12.
St. Francis Winery, on the right, greets you in a few hundred feet. This

winery, on one hundred acres, was established in 1979 and is renowned for estate grown Merlots and Chardonnays.

Turn right from St. Francis and you'll soon see *Smothers Brothers Winery.* Yes, it's the famous comedy team. This winery has a sense of humor but takes wine making seriously, with award-winning Chardonnays, Merlots, and Cabernets.

Proceed south about a mile and turn right onto Dunbar Lane. *Wellington Vineyards* will be on your right in $^1/_2$ mile. Operated by John Wellington and his son, Peter, since 1989, it specializes in red wines, about half of which include the grapes from the hundred-year-old vines at the estate.

Continue on Dunbar Lane until it runs into Arnold Drive, in about 2 miles; turn right and you're almost in Glen Ellen. If you started in Sonoma, retrace your path from there.

WINERIES

Chateau St. Jean, 8555 Sonoma Highway, Kenwood 95452.
(707) 833-4134. Daily, 10:00–4:30.

Kenwood Vineyards, 9592 Sonoma Highway, Kenwood 95452.
(707) 833-5891. Daily, 10:00–4:30.

Landmark Vineyards, 101 Adobe Canyon Road, Kenwood 95452.
(707) 833-0053. Daily, 10:00–4:30.

Matanzas Creek Winery, 6097 Bennett Valley Road, Santa Rosa 95404.
(707) 528-6464. Monday–Saturday, 10:00–5:00;
Sundays, 11:00-5:00.

St. Francis Winery, 8450 Sonoma Highway, Kenwood 95452.
(707) 833-4666. Daily, 10:00–4:30.

Smothers Brothers Winery, 9575 Sonoma Highway, Kenwood 95452.
(707) 833-1010. Daily, 10:00–4:30.

Wellington Vineyards, 11600 Dunbar Road, Glen Ellen 95442.
(707) 939-0708. Daily, 12 noon–5:00.

STOPPING SITES

Buckley Lodge, 1717 Adobe Canyon Rd., Kenwood. (707) 833-5562.
Daily (except Tuesday), open for lunch and dinner.

Morton's Warm Springs Park, 1651 Warm Springs Road, Kenwood.
(707) 833-5511. Seasonal operation.

Sonoma County

RUSSIAN RIVER AREA

Russian River Area

GETTING THERE *The Russian River area is reached via Highway 101. Take the Guerneville Road exit several miles north of Santa Rosa and head west. Key Map A (page 21) shows the roads you need to take.*

FRIENDLY WINERIES AND GREAT COUNTRY ATMOSPHERE CHARACTERIZE THIS AREA. Apples, another traditional crop, provide incomparable displays of blooms in early spring. The delicious apples are celebrated at the annual Gravenstein Festival in August. In summer this is a popular resort area with swimming opportunities and juicy roadside blackberries that offer great excuses to pause for a rest.

The Russian River wine region follows along from the river north to Cloverdale and includes some of the prime wine growing areas of California. There is great variety in climate and soil even within this small area. Dry Creek and Alexander Valley wines are quite different from those of the cooler Russian River areas that are located south of Healdsburg.

I have divided the area into six rides that can easily be connected for several says of exploration. Distances vary from ten to thirty miles. Each ride is contiguous with at least one other ride so you can link them together for a longer ride. This area gets hot in the summer, so be forewarned and avoid the midday hours. You may also want to ride a shorter distance than you're accustomed to.

PLACES TO STAY

CAMPING

Austin Creek State Recreation Area, 6 miles north of Guerneville on Armstrong Woods Road. (707) 869-2015. Open all year.

Cloverdale KOA, 6 Miles SE of Cloverdale at 26460 River Road. (707) 894-3337.Open all year.

BED AND BREAKFAST

Campbell Ranch Inn, 1475 Canyon Road, Geyserville 95441. (707) 857-3476 or (800) 959-3878. They will provide transportation to local restaurants if you don't want to ride to dinner!

Grape Leaf Inn, 539 Johnson St., Healdsburg 95448. (707) 433-8140.

Wine Country Inns of Sonoma, P.O. Box 51, Geyserville 95441.
(707) 433-4667.

HOTELS

Best Western Dry Creek Inn, 198 Dry Creek Road, Healdsburg 95448.
(707) 433-0300, (800) 222-5784.

Madrone Manor, 1001 Westside Road, Healdsburg 95448.
(707) 433-4231.

BICYCLE ASSISTANCE

Cloverdale Cyclery, 125 N. Cloverdale Blvd., Cloverdale 95425.
(707) 894-2841. Tuesday–Saturday, 10:00-5:30, all year.

Dave's Bike Sport, 353 College Ave., Santa Rosa 95401.
(707) 528-3283. Monday–Friday, 10:00–7:00;
Saturday, 10:00–6:00; Sunday, 10:00–5:00. Rentals available.

Healdsburg Cyclery, 294 Center Street, Healdsburg 95448.
(707) 433-7171. Monday–Friday, 10:00–6:00 (closed Tuesday);
Saturday, 10:00–5:00; Sunday, 11:00–4:00. Rentals available.

Mike's Bikes, 16442 Main Street, Guerneville 95446. (707) 869-1106.
Daily, 9:00–5:00 in summer; closed Tuesday and Wednesday in
winter. Rentals available.

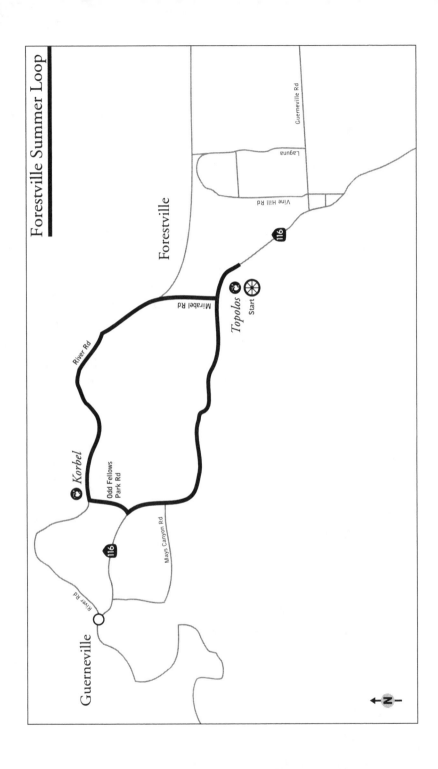

Forestville Summer Loop

❺ Forestville Summer Loop

Short, sweet, bubbly ride with two wineries.

Approximately 10 miles.

STARTING THE RIDE *This ride provides a river crossing in the summer and champagne tasting all year long. • Start your ride at* Topolos at Russian River Vineyards. *To reach it, turn right onto Highway 116 from Guerneville Road, and proceed a few miles. The winery, located at 5700 Gravenstein Highway (Highway 116), will be on your left. The parking lot here is ample. Topolos is happy to have you park your car at the winery, but do make special arrangements if your group has more than one or two cars.*

The Russian River Vineyards Restaurant, at the winery, serves wonderful Greek food in a pleasant outdoor setting. Lunch awaits your return. This winery specializes in classic varietals from old vines, of which their Alicante Bouschet is an outstanding example. Michael Topolos has been at the helm for many years.

From the parking lot, turn left onto Highway 116. Continue for about 1 mile to Mirabel Road, where you turn right. In $1^1/2$ miles turn left onto River Road. This is a busy road, so keep alert. Pedal $2^1/2$ miles to *Korbel Champagne Cellars* on the right. Their excellent tour explains the intricacies of champagne and brandy production.

As you leave the winery, look carefully across River Road and you'll see a tiny road named Odd Fellows Park Road. This road leads through the park and across a bridge that is removed in the winter months. You can stop for a dip in the river here. At the end of Odd Fellows Park Road, in about 1 mile, you'll be at the intersection of Highway 116. Turn left for the last 4 miles to your starting point. Highway 116 is a main road, so heads up.

Plan to go up the road to Kozlowski Farms after lunch to pick up fresh seasonal fruit and legendary preserves. It is one of the many members of Sonoma County Farm Trails, a collective of farms that allow you to pick or purchase seasonal products all over the county. Their annual map also notes local fairs and special events.

In the winter, retrace your steps on River Road after your visit to Korbel, and return the way you came.

WINERIES

Korbel Champagne Cellars, 13250 River Road, Guerneville 95446. (707) 887-2294. Daily, 9:00–4:30.

Topolos at Russian River Vineyards, 5700 Gravenstein Highway, (Hwy. 116), Forestville 95436. (707) 887-1575. Daily, 11:00–5:30.

STOPPING SITES

Kozlowski Farms, 5566 Gravenstein Highway (Highway 116), Forestville 95436. (707) 887-1587.

Russian River Vineyards Restaurant, 5700 Gravenstein Highway, Forestville 95436. (707) 887-1562.

Sonoma County Farm Trails, P.O. Box 6032, Santa Rosa 95406. (707) 996-2154. Order a map by sending a SASE with fifty-five cents postage.

❻ Russian River

Easy eight wineries.

Approximately 18 miles.

STARTING THE RIDE *The highlight of this ride is the variety of the wineries, from down-home to downright elegant. The terrain involves a slight uphill on the return trip; nothing you can't do, though. To get to Dehlinger Winery, the starting point for the ride, turn right off Guerneville Road at Vine Hill Road, just before Highway 116.*

Located on a hillside, *Dehlinger Winery* is picture perfect, with a pleasant, cool tasting room that offers a good selection from the family winery. Park your car at the road since parking at the tasting room is limited. As you leave the driveway, turn left onto Guerneville Road, heading east. Continue about ³/4 mile and turn left onto Laguna Road.

Martini and Prati Winery will be on your left in about 1¹/4 miles. In operation since 1881, this is one of the oldest wineries in Sonoma County. The folks at this winery will greet you warmly, but the resident dog may be a bit too friendly. You can take one of the two daily tours and fill your own jug directly from a barrel, a tradition of this winery. Of course, standard bottles are also available. A left turn as you leave keeps you moving north. In about 1¹/4 miles, turn right on Trenton Road. This is a very sharp turn of about 240 degrees.

Joseph Swan Vineyards tasting room is on the right.(The address of the winery is Laguna Road, but access to the tasting room is here.) Joseph Swan has just replanted one of its vineyards with phylloxera-resistant root stock; check it out for the different ideas that are incorporated. The winery produces several Zinfandels from various vineyards. Double back to Laguna Road as you leave the winery and turn right toward River Road.

Proceed with caution along River Road, a busy road. *Martinelli Vineyards* will be on your right in about 3 miles. In addition to varietal wines, Martinelli also produces the best apple juice and cider, and offers it for tasting. You will want to purchase some of this to refill your water bottle!

Next-door-neighbor *Z Moore Winery* will come into view shortly. Their "penthouse" tasting room offers great views along with excellent Gewürztraminers.

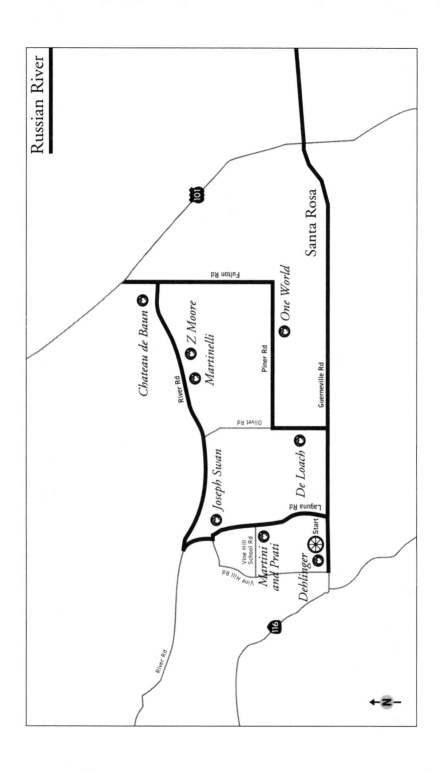

Russian River

Chug along another 2 miles to Fulton Road, where you turn left. In $^1/_4$ mile, *Chateau de Baun* will be on the left. The fabulous chateau that is home to this winery is straight from the French countryside. The winery is available for weddings and other events. It produces several varieties of champagne to fit with the celebratory mode. The grounds are lovely and invite you to linger with a picnic.

Turn right onto Fulton Road as you leave the winery and head south. Ride 2 $^3/_4$ miles to Piner Road and turn right. After 1 mile you will see *One World Winery* on the left. This small, specialty winery, with attitude, is open on weekends. Its intent is to produce affordable, quality wines. A noble goal!

Olivet Road intersects in 1 $^1/_2$ miles. Turn left here and ride $^3/_4$ mile to *De Loach Vineyards*. This family operation produces award winning varietals. You can picnic among the vines. Turn right and continue south as you leave the winery. In 1 mile you'll be at Guerneville Road. Turn right and pedal along the slight uphill 2 miles to Dehlinger Winery.

WINERIES

Chateau de Baun, 5007 Fulton Road, Fulton 95439.
   (707) 571-7500. Daily, 10:00–5:00.
Dehlinger Winery, 6300 Guerneville Road, Sebastopol 95472.
   (707) 823-2378. Daily, 10:00–5:00.
De Loach Vineyards, 1791 Olivet Road, Santa Rosa 95401.
   (707) 526-9111. Daily, 10:00–4:30.
Joseph Swan Vineyards, 2916 Laguna Road, Forestville 95436.
   (707) 573-3747. Daily, 11:00–4:30.
Martinelli Vineyards, 3360 River Road, Windsor 95492.
   (707) 525-0570. Daily, 10:00–5:00.
Martini and Prati Winery, 2191 Laguna Road, Santa Rosa 95401.
   (707) 575-8064. Daily, 11:00–4:00.
One World Winery, 2948 Piner Road, Santa Rosa 95401.
   (707) 525-0390. Weekends only, 10:30–4:00 or by appointment.
Z Moore Winery, 3364 River Road, Windsor 95492.
   (707) 544-3555. Daily, 10:00–5:00.

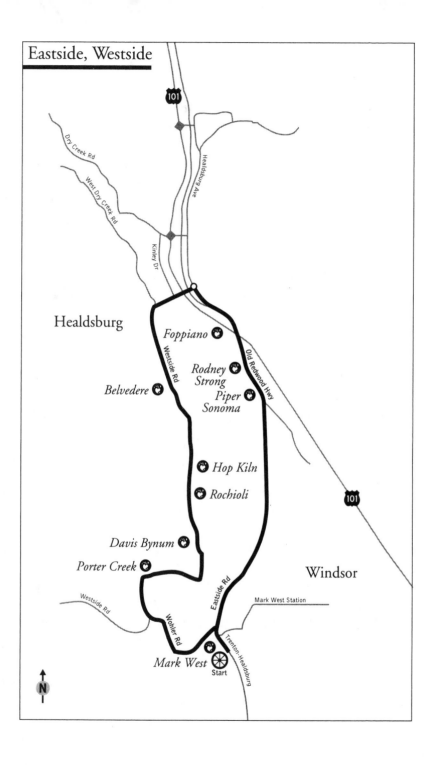

Eastside, Westside

101

Dry Creek Rd

West Dry Creek Rd

Kinley Dr

Healdsburg Ave

Healdsburg

Foppiano

Rodney Strong

Westside Rd

Belvedere

Piper Sonoma

Old Redwood Hwy

Hop Kiln

Rochioli

Davis Bynum

Porter Creek

101

Windsor

Westside Rd

Mark West Station

Wohler Rd

Eastside Rd

Trenton-Healdsburg

Mark West
Start

N

⑦ Eastside, Westside

Nine wineries with lots of variety.

Approximately 19 miles.

STARTING THE RIDE *To get to* Mark West Winery, *located at 7010 Trenton-Healdsburg Road, go west on Guerneville Road from Highway 101 and turn right in about 5 miles at Laguna. Head north and cross River Road, where the road changes names to Trenton-Healdsburg Road. You'll spot the winery on your left in a few miles. This ride takes you up one side of the Russian River and down along the other side. The terrain is beautiful.*

Your ride to Healdsburg starts at the lovely *Mark West Estate Vineyard and Winery.* This winery grows all its grapes organically and makes fine Chardonnay, Gewürztraminer, and Pinot Noir. It is consistent in its organic approach and even makes use of recycled materials in its packing boxes. The picnic area commands a great view and, with prior arrangement, can accommodate groups. A left turn from the driveway puts you on Trenton-Healdsburg Road. In about ¹/₂ mile, this becomes Eastside Road. Continue north and enjoy the countryside.

In about 5 miles, you'll be at the intersection of Old Redwood Highway, the site of *Piper Sonoma.* Stop here for a taste of sparkling wine on the terrace of this state-of-the-art facility.

A few pedals along Old Redwood Highway and you'll see *Rodney Strong Vineyards* on your left. Take a guided tour or just enjoy the latest display in the art gallery. Oak-aged wines are a specialty.

Ride another 1¹/₂ miles and on your left will be *Foppiano Vineyards.* Founded in 1896, the fifth generation is now operating this winery. Its trademark product is Petite Sirah, which has been produced for almost one hundred years. You can stretch your legs with a self-guided walking tour through the vineyards.

Turn left as you leave and continue north on Old Redwood Highway another 1¹/₂ miles, then make a left turn to Westside Road. The lovely Victorian house that is the home of *Belvedere Winery* will be on your right in about 3 miles. Belvedere produces wines from the selected areas of Alexander Valley, Dry Creek, and the Russian River Valley. You're invited to picnic in the garden.

43

Another 2 miles down Westside Road, you'll spot *Hop Kiln Winery* on your left. The three-towered hop barn, an echo of the former crop of the region, is the symbol and name of this winery.

Next door is the *Rochioli Vineyard and Winery*, which produces fine wine from its own vineyard. It also features art shows.

A bit shy of 2 miles further, you'll see *Davis Bynum Winery* on your right. Follow the driveway along the canyon to the barn, where you can taste the wide range of wines made by father and son Bynum team, Davis and Hampton.

Less than $^1/4$ mile, again on your right will be the idyllic setting of *Porter Creek Vineyards*. Taste Pinot Noir and Chardonnay next door in the lovely farmhouse. Continue on Westside Road another $^1/2$ mile and turn left onto Wohler Road. Proceed on Wohler about 1 mile; then turn left onto Eastside Road. In about 1 mile, turn right onto Trenton-Healdsburg Road and head back to Mark West Winery where you began, it's about $^1/2$ mile.

WINERIES

Belvedere Winery, 4035 Westside Road, Healdsburg 95448. (707) 433-8236. Daily, 10:00–4:30.

Davis Bynum Winery, 8075 Westside Road, Healdsburg 95448. (707) 433-2611. Daily, 10:00–5:00.

Foppiano Vineyards, 12707 Old Redwood Highway, Healdsburg 95448. (707) 433-7272. Daily, 10:00–4:30.

Hop Kiln Winery, 6050 Westside Road, Healdsburg 95448. (707) 433-6491. Daily, 10:00–5:00.

Mark West Estate Winery, 7010 Trenton-Healdsburg Road, Forestville 95436. (707) 544-4813. Daily, 10:00–5:00.

Piper Sonoma, 11447 Old Redwood Highway, Healdsburg 95448. (707) 433-8843. Daily, 10:00–5:00.

Porter Creek Vineyards, 8735 Westside Road, Healdsburg 95448. (707) 433-6321. Daily, 10:30–4:30.

Rochioli Vineyard and Winery, 6192 Westside Road, Healdsburg 95448. (707) 433-2305. Daily 10:00–5:00, except 11:00–4:00 in December and January.

Rodney Strong Vineyards, 11455 Old Redwood Highway, Healdsburg 95448. (707) 431-1533. Daily, 10:00–5:00.

❽ Dry Creek

Nice, mostly flat, countryside with six wineries.

Approximately 14 miles.

STARTING THE RIDE *This ride is a great introduction to the area with some nice cycling. Take Highway 101 north to the Central Healdsburg exit. Key Map A (page 21) shows the way. • Start this ride early in the day, and save exploration of the town for the afternoon. It gets really hot out on the roads. Park near the corner of Healdsburg Avenue and Dry Creek Road.*

Head out of town on Dry Creek Road; within minutes you're in the country. In about 5 miles, Lytton Springs intersects Dry Creek Road. Stay on Dry Creek Road another ¹/₂ mile and turn left onto Lambert Bridge Road.

A few hundred feet will find you with a choice of wineries. *Robert Stemmler Vineyards*, on the right, specializes in award-winning Pinot Noirs. *Dry Creek Vineyard*, on your left, was founded in 1972 and has established itself as a premium producer of classically styled red and white varietal wines.

Return to Lambert Bridge Road, continuing west. The road winds around a bit here, so be careful to stay on it another ¹/₂ mile to the intersection of West Dry Creek Road.

Turn left again and proceed south. In about ¹/₄ mile, on your right, you'll see the distinctive building that houses *Lambert Bridge Winery*. This winery was founded in 1975 and makes excellent Chardonnay and Merlot. The interior of the building is a work of art and provides a soothing atmosphere for tasting.

Turn right as you leave and continue south on West Dry Creek; in 3³/₄ miles the elegant *Bellerose Vineyard* will be on your right. This winery is family owned and creates Bordeaux-style wines.

Another ¹/₂ mile brings you to the intersection of Westside Road; turn left here, and in about ¹/₂ mile you'll run into Healdsburg Avenue. Turn left and head north through town to your starting point.

Or, stop to explore the shops, restaurants, and additional wineries that are in the town of Healdsburg. The wineries are easy to locate from

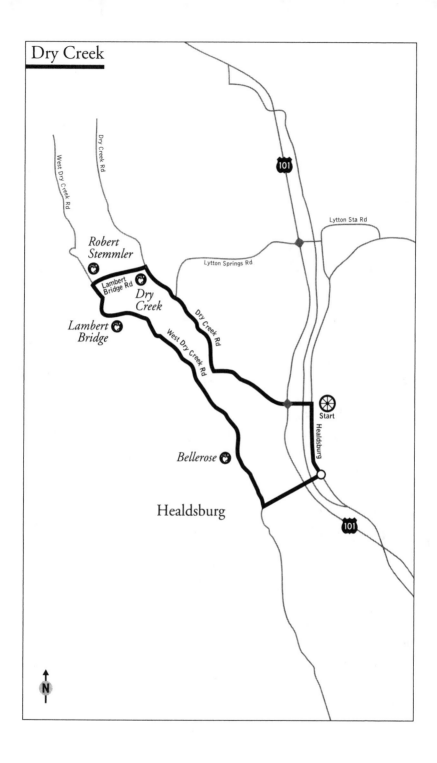

the signposts in town and are listed below. If you're ready for a casual meal try Lo Spuntino, a new deli with an Italian accent and a wine bar. For a treat try Sweets from the Heart.

WINERIES

Alderbrook Winery, 2306 Magnolia Drive, Healdsburg 95448. (707) 433-9154. Daily, 10:00–5:00.

Bellerose Vineyard, 435 West Dry Creek Road, Healdsburg 95448. (707) 433-1637. Daily, 11:00–4:30.

Dry Creek Vineyard, 3770 Lambert Bridge Road, Healdsburg 95448. (707) 433-1000. Daily, 10:30–4:30.

Kendall-Jackson, 337 Healdsburg Ave., Healdsburg 95448. (707) 433-7102. Daily, 10:00–4:30.

Lambert Bridge Winery, 4085 West Dry Creek Road, Healdsburg 95448. (707) 431-9600. Daily, 10:00–5:00.

Robert Stemmler Vineyards, 3805 Lambert Bridge Road, Healdsburg 95448. (707) 433-6334. By appointment, 10:00–4:30.

STOPPING SITES

Lo Spuntino, 400 First Street East, Healdsburg 95448. (707) 935-5656. Open daily.

Sweets from the Heart, 340 Healdsburg Avenue, Healdsburg 95448. (707) 433-1807. Monday–Saturday, 10:00–9:00; Sunday, 12 noon–6:00.

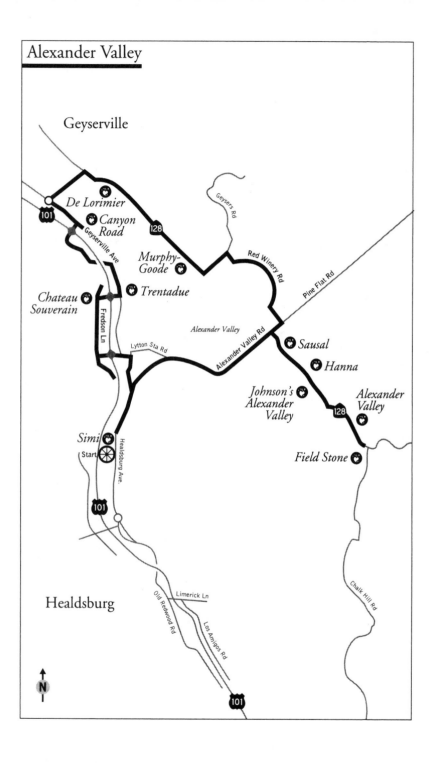

Alexander Valley

Geyserville

De Lorimier

101

Canyon Road

Geyserville Ave.

128

Geysers Rd

Red Winery Rd

Pine Flat Rd

Murphy-Goode

Trentadue

Chateau Souverain

Fredson Ln

Lytton Sta Rd

Alexander Valley

Alexander Valley Rd

Sausal

Hanna

Johnson's Alexander Valley

128

Alexander Valley

Simi

Start

Healdsburg Ave.

Field Stone

101

Healdsburg

Old Redwood Rd

Limerick Ln

Los Amigos Rd

Chalk Hill Rd

101

N

❾ Alexander Valley

Winding through the Alexander Valley with eleven wineries.

Approximately 30 miles.

STARTING THE RIDE *This ride begins at* Simi Winery, *just outside of Healdsburg, at 16275 Healdsburg Ave. • Take Highway 101 north to Healdsburg, and exit at Central Healdsburg. Key Map A (page 21) shows the way. The ride will acquaint you intimately with the factors that give the Alexander Valley such a special microclimate.*

At *Simi Winery,* the old stone winery is still in use. This is, however, a modern facility with a full range of wines and a lovely picnic area. Turn left from the parking lot. Keep to the right, and you'll soon be on Alexander Valley Road.

In about $4\,^3/_4$ miles, you will be at the intersection of Highway 128. Just before the intersection, you'll pass by the Jimtown Store. Its name harks back to the original town name.

Highway 128 is a main road, so be cautious. Turn right, and in about 2 miles, you'll see *Johnson's Alexander Valley Wines* on the right. This is a very small family winery where daughter Ellen Johnson is the wine maker.

A right turn as you leave, and another 2 miles, will land you at *Field Stone Winery.* You pass by an impressive array of barrels on the way to the intimate tasting room. This small winery makes BIG bottles of wine, as in Jeroboams, Methuselahs, Salmanazars and Nebuchadnezzars, that are great for aging. The largest size will serve a party of forty or fifty, so you'd better have a strong arm on hand to pour the wine!

From the winery, turn left and head back along Highway 128. In about $2^1/_2$ miles, *Alexander Valley Vineyards* will be on the right. This twenty-year-old winery is still family-run. Most of their wines are estate-bottled reds that thrive in the warm microclimate of the Alexander Valley.

Less than one mile farther, again on the right, and you'll be at the foot of the long driveway winding through the vineyard to the *Hanna Winery* tasting room. Cabernets and Merlots are featured. The new wine maker, Jon Engelskirger, has big plans which include a Reserve Sauvignon Blanc.

Turn right as you depart the driveway, and *Sausal Winery* will greet you on the right in another 1 1/2 miles. Founded in 1973 by the Demostene family, this winery makes outstanding estate-bottled Zinfandels along with other varietals.

Turn right, leaving the winery, and continue about 1/4 mile. Swing right for a brief stay on Pine Flat Road, then turn left onto Red Winery Road and enjoy the countryside. The road ends in about 2 1/2 miles, at Geysers Road.

Turn left, and in about 1/2 mile you'll see Highway 128; head right and proceed north. *Murphy-Goode Estate Winery* will be on the left in about 1/4 mile. This winery is a partnership of grape growers Tim Murphy and Dale Goode. Fumé Blanc is their flagship wine.

Continue on Highway 128 for 2 more miles, and *De Lorimier Winery* will be on the left. It produces estate blends to obtain more complex characteristics than are possible with a varietal. For a wine to be labeled a varietal at least seventy-five percent of the grapes must be of that variety. De Lorimier's aim is to have wines identified more by their place of origin than by the type of grape used. This is more akin to the European designations.

This winery caters to bicyclists by offering to ship wines anywhere in California or Oregon for ten dollars per case, lots better than carrying the wine on your rack! Return to Highway 128 and follow the signs heading northwest, left, 2 miles into the quaint town of Geyserville.

Once in town, make a left turn and head south on Geyserville Road; it is a frontage Road to Highway 101. (The next 7 miles you'll be skirting the highway.) On your left in about 3 miles, *Canyon Road Winery*, owned by Geyser Peak, offers a complete range of wines. You can also join them at their traditional crush party in the fall.

Trentadue Winery follows in 1 mile. Started in 1972 by Leo Trentadue, the old 32 winery carries on in the Italian tradition of good wine at a fair price. This friendly facility offers a free gondola ride through the vineyards. Take special note of the red wines, which are produced from old stock vines.

Take Independence Lane, directly across from the winery as you exit. At the turn in the road, in about 1/2 mile, is *Chateau Souverain*. This elegant facility offers a complete range of wines. The restaurant is superb; a summer lunch on the terrace overlooking the Alexander Valley is heavenly.

As you leave the winery, turn right and cycle down Fredson Lane about $1^1/_2$ miles to the intersection of Lytton Springs Road. Turn left here, passing under Highway 101, and turn right in less than 1 mile onto Healdsburg Avenue. In $2^1/_4$ miles, *Simi Winery* will be on your right.

WINERIES

Alexander Valley Vineyards, 8644 Highway 128, Healdsburg 95448. (707) 433-7209. Daily, 10:00–5:00.

Canyon Road Winery, 19950 Geyserville Avenue, Geyserville 95441. (707) 857-3417. Daily, 10:00–5:00.

Chateau Souverain, 400 Souverain Road, Geyserville 95441. (707) 433-8281. Daily, 10:00–5:00.

De Lorimier Winery, 2001 Highway 128, Geyserville 95441. (707) 433-7718. Friday–Monday, 10:00–4:00.

Field Stone Winery, 10075 Highway 128, Healdsburg 95448. (707) 433-7266. Daily, 10:00–5:00.

Hanna Winery, 9280 Highway 128, Healdsburg 95448. (707) 575-3330. Daily, 10:00–4:00.

Johnson's Alexander Valley Wines, 8333 Highway 128, Healdsburg 95448. (707) 433-2319. Daily, 10:00–5:00.

Murphy-Goode Estate Winery, 4001 Highway 128, Geyserville 95441. (707) 431-7644. Daily, 10:30–4:30.

Sausal Winery, 7370 Highway 128, Healdsburg 95448. (707) 433-2285. Daily, 10:00–4:00.

Simi Winery, 16275 Healdsburg Avenue, Healdsburg 95448. (707) 433-6981. Daily, 10:00–4:30.

Trentadue Winery, 19170 Geyserville Avenue, Geyserville 95441. (707) 433-3104. Daily, 10:00–5:00.

STOPPING SITES

Chateau Souverain Cafe, 400 Souverain Road, Geyserville. (707) 433-3141. Friday–Sunday, open for lunch and dinner.

Jimtown Store, 6706 Highway 128, Healdsburg. (707) 433-1212.

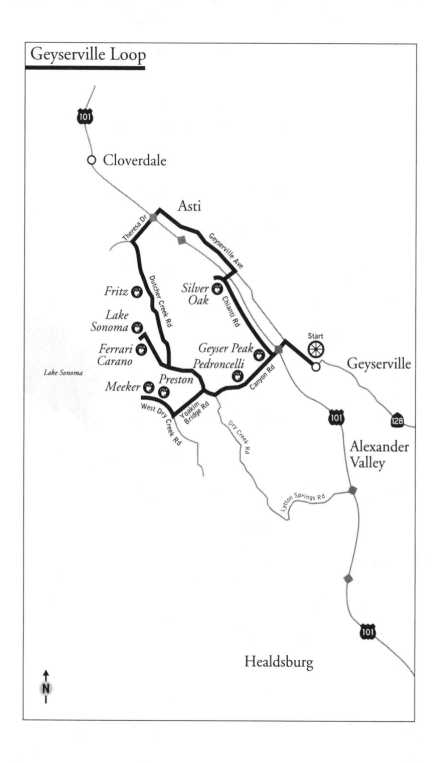

Geyserville Loop

⑩ Geyserville Loop

Eight remote wineries with an optional hill.

Approximately 27 miles.

STARTING THE RIDE *The riding on this country route is close to perfect; in fact, part of this ride is the course used for an annual bike race. Start the ride on Geyserville Avenue where it intersects Highway 128. To get to that intersection, take Highway 101 north to Geyserville; exit at the first Geyserville exit. Key map A (page 21) shows the way.*

Head north on Geyserville Avenue ¹/₂ mile to Canyon Road and turn left proceeding under Highway 101. Turn right at Chianti Road.

Geyser Peak Winery will be on the left in a few hundred feet. It has a selection of special wines only available at the winery. The picnic area, with a view of the Alexander Valley, welcomes visitors.

Turn left as you depart and continue on Chianti another 2¹/₂ miles to the *Silver Oak Cellars.* This winery produces only world-class Cabernets. There is a charge for tastings, but it is applied to any purchase you make.

Turn right, leaving the winery, then go left in a few pedals to pass under Highway 101. Turn left and continue north on Geyserville Road. In 2¹/₂ miles you'll be at Theresa Drive. Turn left here and then, in ¹/₂ mile, left again. You'll be heading south on Dutcher Creek Road. In 2 miles, *J. Fritz Winery* will be on your right. This futuristic underground winery incorporates energy conservation into each part of the wine making. They also use a unique gravity system to produce free-run juice for their remarkable wine. Gravity flow eliminates pumping and inadvertent aeration of developing wines.

Turn right as you leave the winery and head south another 2 miles to where Dutcher Creek Road intersects Dry Creek Road. Turn right and continue up Dry Creek Road about 1¹/₂ miles to *Lake Sonoma Winery.* It has excellent wines and a good food selection that you can enjoy on the veranda or in the shaded picnic areas. If you're in the mood to keep climbing, continue up the hill for a look at the dam that created Lake Sonoma. If not, turn left from the winery and double back along Dry Creek Road.

In 1 mile *Ferrari-Carano Winery* will be on the right. This winery produces classic varietals from the grapes of the Alexander and Dry Creek valleys.

Turn right as you leave and continue for 1½ miles on Dry Creek Road, then turn right onto Yoakim Bridge Road. Ride 1 mile then turn right again onto West Dry Creek Road.

In about ½ mile, *Preston Winery* will be on your right. This is a family-owned wine estate producing Sauvignon Blanc, Zinfandel, Semillion and Barbera wines, to name a few. They also have a bocce area.

Turn right after your visit and proceed to the end of the road, where you will find *The Meeker Vineyards*. From a charming, remote setting this small family winery has become a premier producer of Zinfandels.

From the end of Dry Creek Road, pedal back to the intersection of Yoakim Bridge Road and turn left. After ½ mile on Yoakim Bridge Road, make another right turn for a brief distance on Dry Creek Road. Turn left onto Canyon Road. *Pedroncelli Winery,* on your left in about 2 miles, will be your next stop. This winery has been in the family since 1927. Sons John and Jim carry on the operation with an accent on varietals.

Turn left onto Canyon Road, proceed through the Highway 101 underpass, and turn right onto Geyserville Avenue. Your starting point is in about 1 mile.

WINERIES

Ferrari-Carano Winery, 8761 Dry Creek Road, Healdsburg 95448.
(707) 433-6700. Daily, 10:00–5:00.

Geyser Peak Winery, 22281 Chianti Road, Geyserville 95441.
(707) 857-9400. Daily, 10:00–5:00.

J. Fritz Winery, 24691 Dutcher Creek Road, Cloverdale 95425.
(707) 894-3389. Daily, 10:30–4:30.

Lake Sonoma Winery, 9990 Dry Creek Road, Geyserville 95441.
(707) 431-1550. Daily, 10:00–5:00.

The Meeker Vineyards, 9711 West Dry Creek Road, Healdsburg 95448.
(707) 431-2148. Daily, 10:00–4:30.

Pedroncelli Winery, 1220 Canyon Road, Geyserville 95441.
(707) 857-3531. Daily, 10:00–5:00.

Preston Winery, 9282 West Dry Creek Road, Healdsburg 95448.
(707) 433-3372. Daily, 12 noon–4:00.

Silver Oak Cellars, 24625 Chianti Road, Geyserville 95441.
(707) 857-3562. Monday–Friday, 9:00–4:30; Saturday, 10:00–4:30.

Mendocino County

EASTERN MENDOCINO COUNTY

Eastern Mendocino County

G **ETTING THERE** *This region is reached by traveling north on Highway 101. Your first stop is just before you enter Hopland. Key Map A (page 21) shows you the way.*

THE RIDES THROUGH THE EASTERN PART OF MENDOCINO COUNTY WILL SHOW YOU THE BEAUTY OF THE LAND and acquaint you with the small towns that support the agricultural base. The Russian River still flows through here, but the land has a different character than that in Sonoma County. The road network is limited, so a busy road is occasionally the only choice.

These three rides, which can easily be connected, range in distance from 14 to 16 miles. The terrain is not demanding, except for the optional hill in the Ukiah ride.

PLACES TO STAY

CAMPING

Kyen Campground, with year-round sites on Lake Mendocino, is ten miles NE of Ukiah off Route 20. (707) 462-7581. Reservations suggested. Fees up to $14.

BED AND BREAKFAST

Private Reserve Cottage, Milano Winery, 14590 South Highway 101, Hopland 95449. (707) 744-1396 or (800) 564-2582.

Sanford House, 306 South Pine Street, Ukiah 95482. (707) 462-1653.

Thatcher Inn, 13401 South Highway 101, P.O. Box 660, Hopland 95449. (707) 744-1890 or (800) 266-1891.

HOTELS

Best Western Inn Ukiah, 601 Talmage Road, Ukiah 95482. (707) 462-8868.

BICYCLE ASSISTANCE

Dave's Bike Shop, 846 South State Street, Ukiah. (707) 462-3230. Monday–Friday, 9:30–5:30; Saturday 9:00–3:00. Closed Sunday so Dave Minsinger can go for a ride, too. Call for rental information.

Ukiah Schwinn, 178 E. Gobbi, Ukiah. (707) 462-2686. Monday–Saturday, 9:00–6:00. Call for rental information.

Hopland Area

Four or five wineries around a picturesque small town.

Approximately 16^1/$_2$ easy miles • Optional 6 miles along Hwy. 101 for the brave.

STARTING THE RIDE *The look of the land here is different from the earlier rides in this book, much more agricultural. A few rolling hills add interest. To begin this ride, park your car on the street in Hopland.*

Head south on Highway 101 from Hopland to *Milano Winery,* about ^{3}/$_4$ mile. Turn right down the bumpy driveway, which you might consider walking. Don't be surprised if a rather intimidating turkey greets you! After Thanksgiving his appearance is not guaranteed. This small, family operation has quite a loyal following because of their distinctive wines. They also have a rustic guest cottage for rent.

As you leave, turn right and continue south along Highway 101 another mile. Turn left, almost one hundred and fifty degrees, onto East Side Road. In about 1 mile the new tasting facility for *Fetzer Vineyards* will be on your right. This new food and wine center offers a wide selection of Mendocino products. There are lots of handicrafts, as well as edibles, to go along with the fine wines produced by Fetzer. Its wines are among the most renowned from the area.

Turn right as you leave the facility and head north on East Side Road. This is one of the loveliest country roads anywhere, with nice rolling terrain.

In about 6 miles you'll see *Whaler Vineyards* on your right. Ann and Russ Nyborg are the cheerful owners. The sea, their other passion, is reflected in their label, which depicts the ancient Norwegian Viking vessel *Godstag.* Zinfandels are king here, with two distinct estate bottled styles. Complimentary tasting at this winery is by appointment only, so plan ahead.

Turn right and slow pedal ^{1}/$_2$ mile to *Domaine Saint Gregory.* Greg Graziano, the owner/wine maker, produces Bordeaux-style wines under the Saint Gregory label and Italian-style wines under the Monte Volpe label. The total production of twelve thousand cases includes a wide variety. Make an appointment a week in advance to try the wines here.

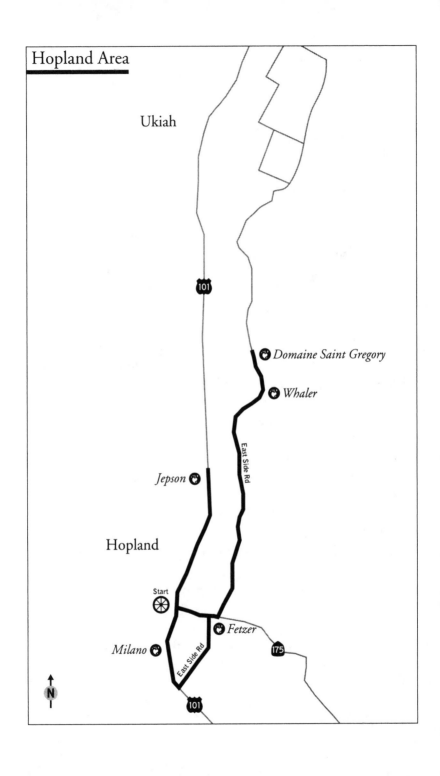

Hopland Area

Ukiah

101

🏵 *Domaine Saint Gregory*

🏵 *Whaler*

East Side Rd

Jepson 🏵

Hopland

Start
✸

🏵 *Fetzer*

175

Milano 🏵

East Side Rd

101

N

A left turn from the driveway starts you south. You'll be back in Hopland in about 7 miles. Take a right on Highway 175 to reach the center of town.

If fast traffic and a narrow shoulder do not deter your willingness to explore further, take this next loop from Highway 101, the main street of Hopland.

Turn north, right, and proceed to *Jepson Vineyards,* about 3 miles from Hopland. Its full range of wines includes estate-bottled whites. The exceptional brandy has earned a place at the White House. Return to Hopland, with caution, along the same route.

Take some time to linger and explore downtown Hopland, which has several inviting antique shops.

If you're ready for a meal, the Blue Bird Cafe is a great local eatery with a 1950s diner ambiance. For more substantial fare, The Hopland Brewery and Restaurant serves lunch and dinner along with their famous Red Tail Ale. Live music is featured Saturday night.

WINERIES
Domaine Saint Gregory, 4921 East Side Road, Ukiah 95482.
(707) 463-1532. Open by appointment only.
Fetzer Vineyards, 13601 East Side Road, Hopland 95449.
(707) 744-1250. Daily, 10:00–5:00.
Jepson Vineyards, 10400 South Highway 101, Ukiah 95482.
(707) 468-8936. Daily, 10:00–5:00.
Milano Winery, 14594 South Highway 101, Hopland 95449.
(707) 744-1396. Daily, 10:00–5:00.
Whaler Vineyards, 6200 East Side Road, Ukiah 95482.
(707) 462-6355. Open by appointment only.

STOPPING SITES
Blue Bird Cafe, 13340 South Highway 101, Hopland.
(707) 744-1633. Open daily.
The Hopland Brewery and Restaurant, 13351 South Highway 101,
Hopland. (707) 744-1361. Open daily.

Rambling Round Ukiah

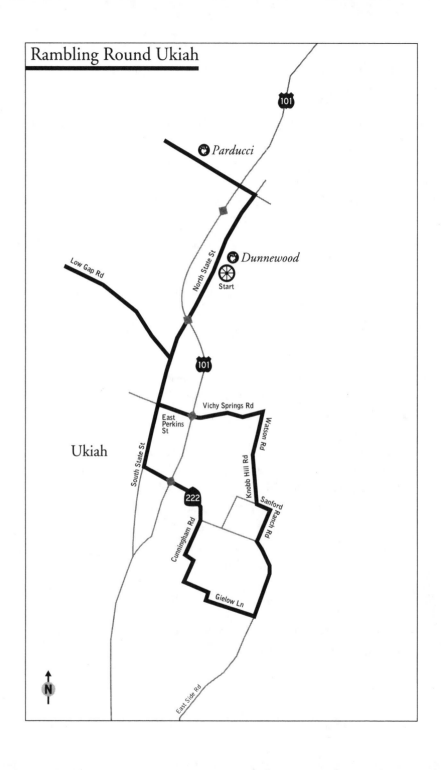

Rambling Round Ukiah

Two wineries and thousands of vines.

Approximately 16 miles • 20 miles with the optional hill detour.

STARTING THE RIDE *This ride is lots of fun with surprises that greet you along the way. Part of the ride goes right through a vineyard.* • *Take Highway 101 north to the North State Street exit in Ukiah. Continue on North State Street to* Dunnewood Vineyards and Winery *at 2399 North State Street.*

The winery welcomes you to park in its lot while you explore. This winery is unique in that it grows no grapes, preferring to leave that to the farmers. It crafts its wines using grapes from each of the four counties that comprise the North Coast region. The lovely picnic area features some rare rhododendrons.

Turn right as you start your ride. In 1¹/₄ mile, turn left onto Parducci Road. In ¹/₂ mile you'll be at the venerable *Parducci Wine Cellars,* which was established in 1932. It prides itself on honest wines that are not processed to the point of masking the flavor. The tasting room offers a wide range of wine-related products as well as a taste of classic wines.

Return to North State Street and turn right. In 2¹/₂ miles, make another right onto Low Gap Road for an optional hill ride. You'll see the town cemetery and various public buildings that are in the heart of Ukiah. The hill, which starts in about ¹/₂ mile, is nicely graded and affords a view of the area that improves as you climb. After 2 miles the pavement ends. That's where I made a U-turn to glide downhill back to North State Street. You could continue on up the hill if your tires and stamina permit.

Turn right onto North State Street and, in about ¹/₂ mile, turn left onto East Perkins Street. Watch out for the railroad tracks. Heads up as you cross at the Highway 101 overpass; the autos trying to go right to the highway have a different agenda than you!

Here the road changes names to Vichy Springs, and you're out in the country. In about 2 miles, Watson Road intersects. Turn right and continue another mile until you get to Knob Hill Road. You get to climb again for a lovely view of the vineyards. In $3/4$ mile you'll have crested the hill and coasted down to the other side.

Turn left on Sanford Ranch Road. You'll be cycling through the vines, splendid! In about $3/4$ mile, Sanford Road becomes East Side Road. To the left you'll see the the entry to the City of 10,000 Buddhas, a Buddhist retreat. In 1 mile, turn right onto Gielow Lane. The only other traffic on this tranquil one-lane road will be a tractor or two.

Turn right at the end of the lane onto Ruddick Cunningham Road, in about $3/4$ mile. Turn left in $1^3/4$ miles and continue into Ukiah on Talmage Road (Highway 222). Turn right in $1^1/4$ miles on South State Street if you're ready to head back to the start.

If you're hungry, Ellie's Mutt Hut and Vegetarian Cafe has a wide selection to satisfy you. If you have a little more ride left, head south on State Street and have lunch at Moores' Flour Mill and Bakery; it's about $1^1/2$ miles. They'll make you a custom sandwich on their organic bread. The water wheel on the porch provides a cool spot for munching.

Stop to check out the typical farm-town stores in Ukiah before you continue north to your starting point, which you will reach $3^1/4$ miles from the intersection of Highway 222.

WINERIES

Dunnewood Vineyards and Winery, 2399 North State Street,
Ukiah 95482. (707) 462-2985. Daily, 10:00–5:00.

Parducci Wine Cellars, 501 Parducci Road, Ukiah 95482.
(707) 462-9463. Daily, 9:00–5:00.

STOPPING SITES

Ellie's Mutt Hut and Vegetarian Cafe, 732 South State Street, Ukiah.
(707) 468-5376. Closed weekends.

Moores' Flour Mill and Bakery, 1550 South State Street, Ukiah.
(707) 462-6550. Closed Sunday.

⓭ Redwood Valley

Charming, rural ride includes three wineries and a real country feel.

Approximately 14 miles.

STARTING THE RIDE *Head up Highway 101 and just past Ukiah, exit at the sign that directs you to Redwood Valley. Turn right onto North State Street. • Several of the wineries here have joined together for a common tasting facility. You can ride to absorb the ambiance and then return to the tasting facility to enjoy a sip of wine.*

The large tasting room for *Redwood Valley Cellars* will be on the left. Several of the wineries of the Redwood Valley share this spacious facility. I suggest you do this ride out into the vineyards first, and then return here for a rest and some samples. The ample parking lot is a fine place to leave your car while you explore.

From the tasting room, turn right and head north on North State Street. In about 1¹/₂ miles, turn right to West Road.

Gabrielli Winery will be on your left in about 4 miles. This is a new winery that bottled its initial production of Zinfandel in 1990. In 1994 it introduced a new white blend, Ascenza. The market for their wines is global; see what you think.

Continue north another mile to the fork in the road. Take the left fork, which is named Tomki Road, and proceed 1³/₄ miles to the *Frey Vineyards*. Organic wine is the specialty here, and there is a real commitment to the environment. Zinfandels are the strong suit, along with Cabernets and Syrahs. The tasting operation has recently been moved to the wine tasting center, but you can still stop and say hello at the winery.

Double back, return to the junction, and turn left onto East Road. You'll be riding through some lovely, unpretentious vineyards. Lilacs perfume the air in the early spring.

You'll pass by *Redwood Valley Vineyards* in about 1 mile. Grapes from this vineyard go into the production of Barra of Mendocino, a wine you will be able to sample at the wine tasting center.

Continue on East Road 2 miles and turn right on Moore Avenue. Cross over the bridge, then turn right again onto North State Street. In 1 mile, you'll be back at the tasting center ready to sample the wines.

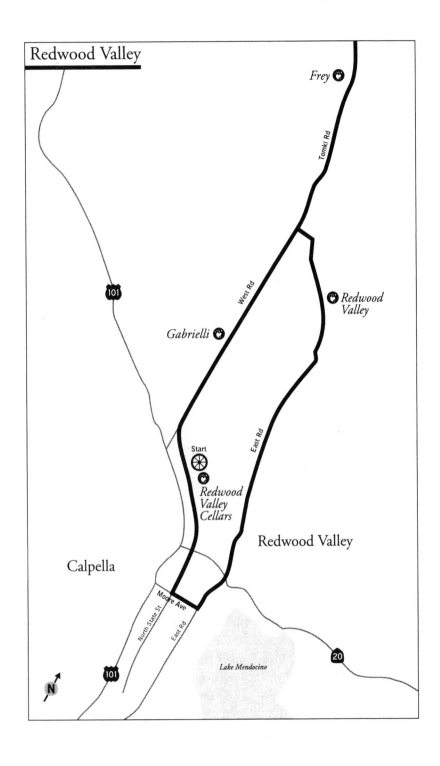

Redwood Valley

Frey

Tomki Rd

101

West Rd

Redwood Valley

Gabrielli

East Rd

Start

Redwood Valley Cellars

Redwood Valley

Calpella

Moore Ave

North State St.

East Rd

101

Lake Mendocino

20

N

There is a lovely picnic area for your enjoyment. Be sure to have a designated driver for the trip home.

WINERIES

Frey Vineyards, 14000 Tomki Road, Redwood Valley 95470.
(707) 485-5177. Open by appointment only.

Gabrielli Winery, 10950 West Road, Redwood Valley 95470.
(707) 485-1221. Daily, 10:00–5:00.

Redwood Valley Cellars, 7051 North State Street, Redwood Valley,
95470. (707) 485-0322. Daily, 9:00–5:00.

Redwood Valley Vineyards, 10801 East Road, Redwood Valley 95470.
Not open to the public. Tastings at Redwood Valley Cellars.

Mendocino County

ANDERSON VALLEY

Anderson Valley

GETTING THERE *From San Francisco it is about one hundred miles to the Anderson Valley. Head north on Highway 101. When you reach Cloverdale, take the turnoff to Highway 128—the exit reads Mendocino/Fort Bragg—heading west toward Boonville. Key Map A (page 21) will direct you. • Western Mendocino County is far more rural than the other areas we explore in this volume. Prepare yourself to be somewhat self-sufficient with water, food, and bike repair items. It could be a long, hot walk. With this rural ambience, there are few roads. This means that bicycles have to share the pavement, which often lacks a good shoulder, with all the other vehicles. Assess your riding abilities and tolerance for traffic as you review these rides.*

THE ANDERSON VALLEY HAS A LONG HISTORY OF WINE MAKING.
The origins were small plantings of grapes European settlers made for their own consumption. These family operations grew to meet the demand of other locals and survived the rigors of Prohibition with "back door" operations. Despite raids by federal agents, some of these wineries survived and have continued in production.

The cooler coastal climate of the Anderson Valley has proven ideal for varietals. You will enjoy the unique quality of Anderson Valley wine, which was awarded its own appellation in 1983.

Grape growing is a significant industry in Mendocino County. Many of the vineyards you will pass produce grapes but do not bottle their own wine. Rumor has it that these grapes end up blended into Napa and Sonoma county wines to round out the flavors with the special taste that cool-weather grapes impart.

Each year, usually the second weekend of June, the Anderson Valley wineries host a barrel tasting weekend. For a modest fee, you purchase a glass and taste wine and complimenting foods at the wineries. Check the website below for further updates.

The two short rides we suggest form one long loop so you can do one section and add on the other for a heartier ride.

PLACES TO STAY

CAMPING

Hendy Woods State Park, 3 miles west of Philo, $^1/_2$ mile off Highway 128 on Greenwood Road. (707) 937-5804. Open all year. Fees are up to $14.00 per night. Reservations are suggested.

Paul Dimmick Campground, 5 miles northwest of Navarro on Highway 128. (707) 937-5804. Open all year. Fees are up to $14.00 per night. Reservations are suggested.

BED AND BREAKFAST

Pottery Inn, 8550 Highway 128, Philo. (707) 895-3069.
The owners cater to cyclists and will give you a ride to dinner. Reserve ahead, especially in summer.

HOTELS

Boonville Hotel, 14040 Highway 128, Boonville. (707) 895-2210.

BICYCLE ASSISTANCE

No bike shops. Boonville has a hardware store, Rossi and Son Hardware, 14200 Highway 128, Boonville. (707) 895-3261.

ADDITIONAL INFORMATION

Anderson Valley Wine Growers have a website. The address is http://www.AVWINES.com.

⑭ North to Navarro

Six wineries to visit out in the backcountry.

Approximately 11 miles.

STARTING THE RIDE *This trip follows along Highway 128, so ride with caution. The road, while not heavily traveled during the week, is narrow, with an insignificant shoulder. I suggest you visit the wineries on your right as you travel along the road. Obviously, you can cross the road and visit them all while you head out and not stop at all in the other direction.*

Start this ride at *Navarro Vineyards*, which is 7 miles north of Boonville. If it is before 11:00 A.M., when the winery opens, park at the side of the road and explore this lovely winery when you return. Navarro does an excellent job of blending local grapes to produce fantastic results. It works with some of the oldest vineyards in the Anderson Valley.

Directly next door is *Greenwood Ridge Vineyards.* The small annual production of about six thousand cases each year means a quick sellout. Established in 1973, Greenwood Ridge produces great varietal wines, each with a distinctive taste created by the unique soil and climate of the Anderson Valley. Five of their wines were award winners in a recent competition.

Head north on this two-lane country road. Scenic hillsides covered with vines make this especially enjoyable.

Ride another ³/₄ mile, and *Roederer Estate* will be on the right. The first vines were planted by Champagne Roederer, the renowned French company, in 1978. The first release was in 1988. Ownership of their vineyards and the addition of oak-aged reserve wines to each year's blend are the two unique elements of the production. The tasting room, completed in 1991, offers award-winning sparkling wines that reflect a two-hundred-year-old tradition.

Turn right as you leave to continue north another mile to *Handley Cellars.* Milla Handley, one of the female pioneers in the wine industry, is the award-winning wine maker. Chardonnay is the signature wine here. Handley also produces three styles of California sparkling wine. The first weekend of each month, the tasting room features a culinary adventure, offering special items that compliment the wine of the month.

Three miles farther down the highway, you'll be in the tiny town of Navarro. Do not blink; you will miss the entire town. The Navarro Store,

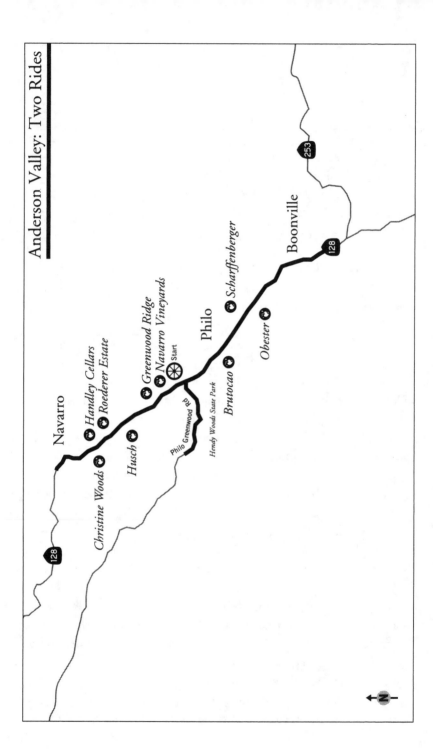

Anderson Valley: Two Rides

Navarro

128

Christine Woods

Handley Cellars
Roederer Estate

Husch

Greenwood Ridge
Navarro Vineyards

Start

Philo Greenwood Rd

Hendy Woods State Park

Philo

Brutocao

Scharffenberger

Obester

Boonville

128

253

N

located at Wendling Street, has cold drinks and organic produce.

Make a U-turn here and explore the wineries on the other side of the road. In about 2 miles the Floodgate Cafe will be on the right. Stop to enjoy the local cuisine in a rustic setting.

Ride on another 1¹/₂ miles to the *Christine Woods Winery.* This winery derives its name from early Swiss settlers in Anderson Valley who called themselves the Christine Community. The Woods part of the name refers to the redwood trees that shade the valley. This exclusive winery, run by the Rose family, produces a scant fifteen hundred cases of estate-bottled Pinot Noir and Chardonnay each year. About half of the grapes are sold to other wineries; the wine is only available at the tasting room.

Continue south 1 mile to *Husch Vineyards,* the oldest winery in the Anderson Valley. This winery was started by a Swede and was bought by the Oswald family when the original owners ran out of heirs. The charming tasting room offers a generous assortment, sharing even its rarest stock, among them the last Cabernet from some very old vines. Most of the production is sold directly from the winery. As with many of the Anderson Valley producers, it will ship to most locations.

Pedal another 1¹/₄ miles to *Navarro,* where you began. If you're ready to ride some more, continue from here with the next ride.

WINERIES

Christine Woods Winery, 3155 Highway 128, Philo 95466.
(707) 895-2115. Daily, 11:00–5:00.

Greenwood Ridge Vineyards, 5501 Highway 128, Philo 95466.
(707) 895-2002. Daily, 10:00–5:00.

Handley Cellars, 3151 Highway 128, Philo 95466. (707) 895-3876.
Daily, 11:00–5:00.

Husch Vineyards, 4400 Highway 128, Philo 95466. (707) 895-3216.
Daily, 10:00–5:00.

Navarro Vineyards, 5601 Highway 128, Philo 95466. (707) 895-3686.
Daily, 11:00–5:00.

Roederer Estate, 4501 Highway 128, Philo 95466. (707) 895-2288.
Daily, 11:00–5:00.

STOPPING SITES

Navarro Store, 231 Wendling, Navarro. (707) 895-3470.
Floodgate Cafe, 1810 Highway 128, Navarro. (707) 895-3988.

⑮ Philo to Boonville

Rolling road with three wineries.

Approximately 14 miles. (See page 70 for map.)

STARTING THE RIDE *Start this ride, which continues from the end of ride 14, across the road from Navarro Vineyards and head south.*

In ¹/₂ mile, turn right onto Greenwood Ridge Road. In about ¹/₂ mile look for the Apple Farm on the left. Here you can taste legendary apple juice and cider. If you've arrived in April, you may even be able to feast on a stunning display of flowering trees. The Hendy Woods State Park is another 2¹/₂ miles out this road.

Retrace your steps back to Highway 128 and continue south. In about ¹/₂ mile, *Brutocao Cellars* will come into view. The tasting room is here, but most of the vineyards are in the Hopland area. This winery, in business since 1980, produces five to ten thousand cases of estate grown red and white classics. Their Cabernet Sauvignon is of special note.

Turn right and continue down the highway another 2 miles, a little past Philo; *Obester Winery* will be on the right. This winery was started in Half Moon Bay by Sandy and Paul Obester and her grandfather, John Gemello, in 1977. The Gemello label is still used on the hearty reds.

Obester, the only certified organic winery in the Anderson Valley, produces Chardonnay, Sauvignon Blanc, and Pinot Noir. In deference to its origins in Half Moon Bay, Obester makes a Pumpkin Festival wine each autumn with collector-quality labels. Samples of their house-made gourmet food products might also be available.

Continue south on Highway 128 through the beautiful country-side another 4 miles to Boonville. This quaint town will pique your curiosity. See if you can find anyone who speaks Boontling, a language invented here. For a sweet snack, try Biscotti Notti. The Boont Berry Farm Store serves lunch and comes highly recommended. Great dinners are available at the Boonville Hotel Restaurant.

Turn north from town to continue the ride. In 5¹/₂ miles you'll be able to stop at *Scharffenberger Cellars*. Founded in 1981 by John Scharffenberger, this was the first producer of sparkling wines to make the Anderson Valley its home. John spent twenty years studying various Northern California locations before selecting the Anderson Valley. His fine wines, made in the traditional *methode champenoise,* justify all the effort.

Continue your journey north, and in about $1^1/2$ miles you'll be back at the starting point.

WINERIES

Brutocao Cellars, 7000 Highway 128, Philo 95466. (707) 895-2152. Daily, 10:00–6:00.

Obester Winery, 9200 Highway 128, Philo 95466. (707) 895-3814. Daily, 10:00–5:00.

Scharffenberger Cellars, 8501 Highway 128, Philo 95466. (707) 895-2957. Daily, 11:00–5:00.

STOPPING SITES

The Apple Farm, 18501 Greenwood Road, Philo. (707) 895-2333. Self-service. Always open.

Biscotti Notti, 14111 Highway 128, Boonville. (707) 895-3038. Thursday–Monday, 11:00–6:00.

Boonville Hotel Restaurant, 14040 Highway 128, Boonville. (707) 895-2210. Daily (except Tuesday), open for dinner from 6:00.

Boont Berry Farm Store, 13981 Highway 128, Boonville. (707) 895-3576. Daily, 9:00–6:00; Saturday, 10:00–6:00; Sunday, 12 noon–5:00.

Hendy Woods State Park. See camping directory, page 68.

Napa County

NORTHERN NAPA VALLEY

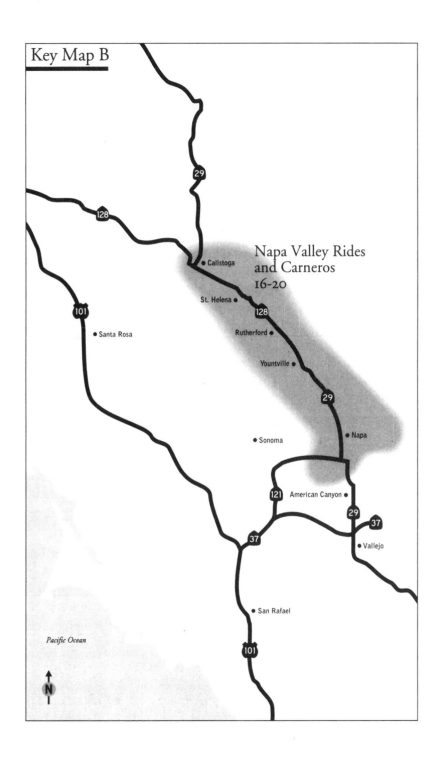

Key Map B

Napa Valley Rides
and Carneros
16-20

• Calistoga

St. Helena •

128

Rutherford •

Yountville •

29

• Sonoma

• Napa

121   American Canyon •

29

37

• Vallejo

37

• San Rafael

Pacific Ocean

N

Northern Napa Valley

GETTING THERE *The rides here begin at the north end of the valley, "Up Valley" in the local jargon. You can start wherever you like. Pick and choose and have fun.* • *If you've been exploring the Alexander Valley, you can continue west on Highway 128; it leads you right into Calistoga. See ride 9 (pages 49–51).* • *If you are coming from San Francisco, take Highway 101 north and turn off at Highway 37. The sign will direct you to Napa/Sonoma. Continue on the highway into Napa, start there or head north on Highway 29 and pick your starting point. Key Map B (page 75) will show you the major roads.*

AT WINERIES IN THE NAPA VALLEY, A SMALL CHARGE FOR TASTING, USUALLY FIVE DOLLARS OR LESS, is the rule rather than the exception, so come prepared. I've made special mention of those that do not charge.

The Napa Valley produces premium wines that are highly regarded throughout the world. To go along with the wine a fabulous food mecca has developed. Be sure to explore at least one of the world class restaurants while you're here.

As you ride through this incredible valley, you will get a sense of the factors that contribute to high quality wine. The geography, the climate, and the talented people are all here for you to investigate. Morning riding is encouraged. The heat and wind, which is usually from the north, are more intense as the day progresses.

I try to keep you off Highway 29 due to the tremendous volume of traffic, especially on the weekends. A few of the rides include a short distance on this road in order to get you to an area of special interest.

The Silverado Trail, our main route through the valley, also has active auto traffic, but it has a broader shoulder more suitable for bicycles. The little roads that cross the valley are especially nice, so you will see at least one of these in each ride, often going out from and back to the Silverado Trail. Once you leave the valley floor the terrain gets quite steep. I've included one optional hill in the text. Many more are available so explore on your own if climbing is your thing.

Napa County has limited the number of wineries that can offer tasting to the public on an open basis, so wineries that have been unable to obtain the required permits offer tastings by appointment. You are equally welcome at these wineries, just call first.

The four Napa Valley rides range from 14 to 21 miles and can easily be connected for a more substantial ride, since all have a section on the Silverado Trail.

PLACES TO STAY

CAMPING

Bothe-Napa State Park, 4 miles south of Calistoga off Highway 29. (707) 942-4575. Open all year. Up to $14.00 per night.

Napa County Fairgrounds, in Calistoga at 1435 Oak Street. (707) 942-5111. Open all year. $15.00 per night.

Skyline Wilderness Park, 2 miles southeast of Napa. Take Imola Avenue and head east. (707) 252-0481. Open all year. $12.00 per night.

BED AND BREAKFAST

Bed and Breakfast Reservation Service for Napa Valley, 1200 Conn Valley Road, St. Helena. (707) 963-4001.

Silver Rose Inn and Spa, 351 Rosedale Road, Calistoga. (707) 942-9581.

HOTELS

Calistoga Inn, 1250 Lincoln Avenue, Calistoga. (707) 942-4101.

Comfort Inn, 1865 Lincoln Avenue, Calistoga. (707) 942-9400.

Hotel St. Helena, 1309 Main Street, St. Helena. (707) 963-4388.

Meadowood Resort, 900 Meadowood Lane, St. Helena. (707) 963-3646. Stay here if money is really no object and you want world-class pampering.

Napa Valley Lodge, 2230 Madison, Yountville. (707) 944-2468.

Sheraton Inn, 3425 Solano Avenue, Napa. (707) 253-7433.

BICYCLE ASSISTANCE

St. Helena Cyclery, 1156 Main Street, St. Helena. (707) 963-7736. Daily, 9:30–5:30; Sundays, 10:00–5:00. Sales, service, rentals. Delivery available.

Palisades Mountain Sport, 1330B Gerrard, Calistoga. (707) 942-9687. Daily, 10:00–6:00. Sales, service, rentals.

Bicycle Works, 3335 Solano in Redwood Plaza, Napa. (707) 253-7000. Tuesday–Friday, 10:00–6:00 (Thursday until 9:00); Saturday, 9:00–5:00. Sales and full repair shop.

Napa Valley Cyclery, 4080 Byway East, at Trower, Napa. (707) 255-3377.Monday–Saturday, 9:00–6:00; Sunday 10:00–4:00. Sales, service, rentals, and tours by reservation.

ADDITIONAL INFORMATION

Napa Valley Virtual Visit website: http://www.napavalley.com/cgi-bin/home.o

Calistoga

Easy ride with Old Faithful and eight wineries.

About 21 miles.

STARTING THE RIDE *This easy tour gives a you good Napa Valley overview and includes the charming town of Calistoga.* • *From Highway 29, turn onto Tubbs Lane. The first winery is* Chateau Montelena, *which is at the east end of Tubbs Lane on the north side. Park in the parking lot closest to the road.*

The fine stone building that houses *Chateau Montelena* is not easily seen from the road. The recently remodeled tasting room is on the upper level. In 1976 the Chardonnay from this winery turned heads at a tasting in Paris by winning a top rating, and the French have not been able to ignore the Napa Valley since then! All of Chateau Montelena's fine wines are estate grown. The climate, soil, and geography combine here at the foot of Mount St. Helena to create an environment ideal for Cabernet Sauvignon. See for yourself.

A right turn as you leave the winery starts you toward the Old Faithful Geyser of California, which you reach in ¹/₂ mile. The Old Faithful designation is rare indeed and indicates a geyser that erupts at regular intervals, in this case once every 40 minutes, over a long period of time. The underground activity that feeds the geyser is also at the heart of the mineral springs that made Calistoga famous as a health resort and source of healing water long before wine became an attraction.

Almost directly across the street will be Myrtledale. Go south on it to continue this ride.

In ¹/₂ mile, turn left to Greenwood Avenue. In another ¹/₂ mile, *Arroyo Winery* will be on the left. This small winery produces estate wines of which Petite Sirah is the signature product. Their exclusive wines, with production of four thousand cases a year, can only be purchased at the winery. Tasting is free.

Continue on Greenwood about ¹/₄ mile to highway 29. Pedal a mile along this relatively sane stretch of the highway until you reach the Silverado Trail, a slight turn to the left.

The Calistoga Mineral Water Company will be on your right. This

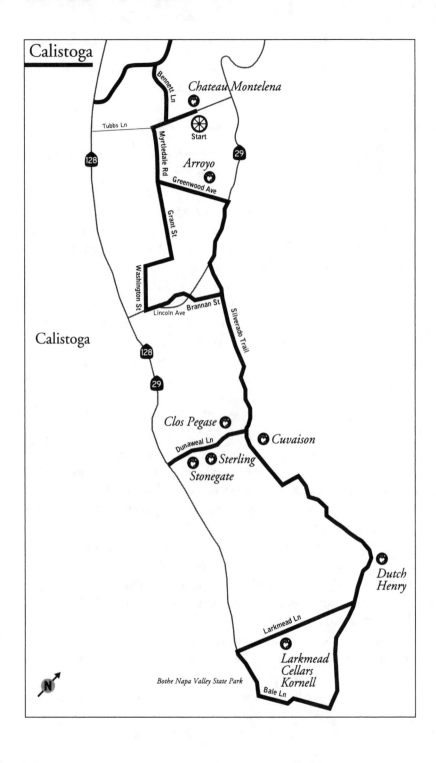

Calistoga

Chateau Montelena

Bennett Ln

Tubbs Ln

Myrtledale Rd

Start

128

29

Arroyo

Greenwood Ave

Grant St

Washington St

Lincoln Ave   Brannan St

Silverado Trail

Calistoga

128

29

Clos Pegase

Dunaweal Ln

Cuvaison

Sterling

Stonegate

Dutch
Henry

Larkmead Ln

N

Bothe Napa Valley State Park

Larkmead
Cellars
Kornell

Bale Ln

local product has been around for years and predates the current bottled water craze. They do not have tours. A viewing window can be reached via the path to the right of the front door. The bottling line, which is most active before 2:00 P.M., will be visible.

You're now on the Silverado Trail. Enjoy the ambiance for 1 1/2 miles. Turn right at Dunaweal Lane for three wineries.

In 1/4 mile, *Clos Pegase Winery* will be on the right. The modern winery design was the result of a national competition. The history of wine making is reflected in artwork that adorns the interior. The graceful atmosphere will enhance your tasting of premium wines.

Almost directly across the road is *Sterling Vineyards,* famous for the aerial tramway that carries you to the winery. The view of the valley from the tram is exceptional. Sterling is celebrating twenty-five years in business as of this writing. Join them in the celebration.

Continue another 1/4 mile to *Stonegate Winery,* almost at the end of the lane on the left. This winery was started in 1973 by the Spaulding family, which is still in charge. The grapes obtained from close-by vineyards are used to make noteworthy Merlot and Cabernet Sauvignons. Tasting is free during the week, with a modest charge on weekends.

After your visit, turn right to retrace your path back to the Silverado Trail. Turn right and continue south.

Cruise along for about 4 miles to Bale Lane. Turn right and cross the valley, it's a little more than 1/2 mile.

Turn right and ride on Highway 29, the shoulder here is quite wide. In about 3/4 mile you'll be at Larkmead Lane.

Turn right here and proceed 1/2 mile to *Larkmead Cellars Kornell.* At fifty years, this is the oldest producer of sparkling wines in the Napa Valley. Tours are available at set times, so call ahead. A friendly greeting and a complimentary taste of excellent champagne are offered when you arrive.

Turn right, leaving the charming grounds to continue on Larkmead Lane. In about 1/2 mile, the Silverado Trail intersects. Turn left and head north.

In 3/4 mile a small sign will direct you to the tiny *Dutch Henry Winery* on the right. This winery, named for the creek that flows nearby, is very bicycle friendly. Even the resident dog is welcoming. With a total production of only two thousand cases each year, the wine is sold exclusively at the winery. All the grapes used are from Napa, and about fifty percent are estate grown. There is no charge for tasting. Mineral water is available for a small charge.

Continue north toward Calistoga. In less than 1 mile, *Cuvaison Winery* will be on your right. This winery is Swiss owned. It produces a full range of wines with a taste that reflects its unique accent.

In about 1$^{1}/_{2}$ mile, turn left to Brannan Street. Continue about $^{1}/_{2}$ mile then turn left onto Lincoln Avenue, the main street of Calistoga.

If you like excellent baked goods, do not miss Napa Valley Ovens; this new establishment is worth riding at least an extra mile. Fellion's Deli, two doors down, is the place for a hearty sandwich. Calistoga is a friendly town with plenty to fill out your afternoon.

When you're through exploring, look for Washington Street and head north. Turn right at Oak Street; the fairgrounds are here if that's where you're camping. In 3 blocks turn left and head north on Grant, which becomes Myrtledale and continues to Tubbs Lane.

Turn right and you'll be back at Chateau Montelena in $^{1}/_{2}$ mile. If you're not ready to stop yet, turn left at Bennett Lane shortly after you get to Tubbs Lane and ride through the vineyards on this one-lane road, a new definition of single track! Retrace your path back to Tubbs Lane, or you'll end up on Highway 128.

WINERIES

Arroyo Winery, 2361 Greenwood Ave., Calistoga 94515.
(707) 942-6995. Daily, 10:00–4:30.

Chateau Montelena, 1429 Tubbs Lane, Calistoga 94515.
(707) 942-5105. Daily, 10:00–4:00.

Clos Pegase Winery, 1060 Dunaweal Lane, Calistoga 94515.
(707) 942-4981. Daily, 10:30–5:00.

Cuvaison Winery, 4550 Silverado Trail, Calistoga 94515.
(707) 942-6266. Daily, 10:00–5:00.

Dutch Henry Winery, 4310 Silverado Trail, Calistoga 94515.
(707) 942-5771. Daily, 10:00–4:30.

Larkmead Cellars Kornell, 1091 Larkmead Lane, Calistoga 94515.
(707) 942-0859. Daily, 10:00–5:00.

Sterling Vineyards, 1111 Dunaweal Lane, Calistoga 94515.
(707) 942-3344. Daily, 10:30–4:30.

Stonegate Winery, 1183 Dunaweal Lane, Calistoga 94515.
(707) 942-6500. Daily, 10:30–4:30.

STOPPING SITES

Calistoga Mineral Water Company, 865 Silverado Trail, Calistoga.
(707) 942–6295. Best viewing is early in the day, weekdays.

Fellion's Delicatessen, 1359 Lincoln Avenue, Calistoga.
(707) 942-6144. Open daily.

The Geysers, 1299 Tubbs Lane, Calistoga. (707) 942-6463.
Open daily. The Geyser takes no holidays.

Napa Valley Ovens, 1353 Lincoln Avenue, Calistoga. (707) 942-0777.
Open daily, except Wednesday.

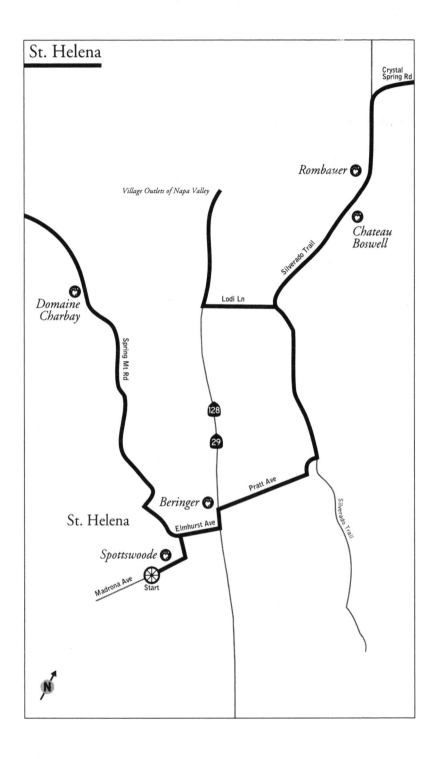

St. Helena

Crystal Spring Rd

Rombauer

Village Outlets of Napa Valley

Silverado Trail

Chateau Boswell

Lodi Ln

Domaine Charbay

Spring Mt Rd

128

29

Pratt Ave

Beringer

Silverado Trail

St. Helena

Elmhurst Ave

Spottswoode

Madrona Ave

Start

N

⑰ St. Helena

Five wineries and a great shopping opportunity • Alternate hill ride for the non-shoppers.

Approximately 13¼ miles • Add 10 miles for the hill option.

STARTING THE RIDE *This ride has a split personality; you can either shop 'til you drop or climb a steep hill 'til you drop. Pick your passion.* • *Start this ride in St. Helena on Madrone Lane. It runs into Highway 29, which is also called the North St. Helena Highway here.*

Park by *Spottswoode Winery* on Madrona Avenue at Hudson Street. Make advance reservations for a complimentary tasting from this small winery. Annual production is nine thousand cases. Tastings are available for up to ten people on Tuesdays at 10:00 A.M. and Fridays at 2:30 P.M.

Head east after your visit, back toward Highway 29. Ride four blocks and turn left on Spring Mountain Road. In two blocks, turn right to Elmhurst, which runs into Highway 29.

Cross Highway 29 carefully as you turn left and then right to the next cross street, Pratt Avenue.

Bisect the valley on this peaceful lane. You'll be at the Silverado Trail in about ¾ mile, total distance from the start will be 1¾ miles.

Turn left and pedal north on the Silverado Trail another 2 miles.

The storybook castle of *Chateau Boswell* will be on your right. Built from hand-hewn blocks of local granite, the interior has the feel of a medieval castle. Currently two wines are produced, a Private Reserve Cabernet Sauvignon and a barrel-fermented Chardonnay. Hours are limited, check first.

Turn right as you depart to continue north. In one mile, turn right on Crystal Springs Road for a small detour into the vineyards. No wineries here, just atmosphere. Keep to the left at the fork in the road unless you want to climb. This little road, North Fork Crystal Springs Road, ends in ¾ mile. Make a U-turn, if you can bear to leave, and head back to the Silverado Trail.

Head south, making a left turn. In ½ mile, *Rombauer Vineyards* is on your right. It's a ¼-mile climb to the winery. Its production includes Carneros Chardonnay and a proprietary red blend named Le Meilleur

85

du Chai. Tastings are complimentary. You deserve no less after climbing the hill!

Continue south ³/₄ mile and make a right turn onto Lodi Lane for the shopping segment. In about ¹/₂ mile, you'll be at Highway 29. Turn right and ride on the shoulder, which is good in this section. There are a couple of wineries here to check out if you choose.

Look carefully to the left, and in ¹/₂ mile the Village Outlets of Napa Valley shopping center will be in view. It is easy to miss. Here you will find a great selection of high quality outlets that include Coach, Donna Karan, and Brooks Brothers. It all goes along with the upscale theme of the Napa Valley. The shops will gladly ship in case you didn't bring your panniers. There is a cafe at the center if you're ready for some food.

Return to Lodi Lane the way you came and continue to the Silverado Trail.

(Although Highway 29 will take you back to St. Helena, the shoulder gets narrow and the traffic is often very busy.)

Head south on the Silverado Trail and in 1 mile, turn right at Pratt Avenue for the ¹/₂ mile back to Highway 29.

If you have not had enough wine yet, cross Highway 29 to visit one of the big boys of the valley, *Beringer*. Its impressive Victorian facility offers a good tour and range of wines to sample. Even Prohibition did not shut down this winery; it continued by making sacramental wines. These are classic Napa Valley wines.

Turn right as you leave the winery and make another right at Elmhurst, the next intersection. In about ¹/₄ mile, you'll be at Spring Mountain Road.

Turn right if you'd like to do a formidable climb up Spring Mountain Road to visit *Domaine Charbay Winery and Distillery*. This steady climb will require low gears, iron legs, or both. The hill brings you through vineyards on a road that is mostly shaded by mature trees. After 4¹/₂ miles, turn left at the next driveway, which will be 4001. Pass the next driveway and continue following the signs to the winery. Do not expect a welcome without prior arrangement. The Karakasevic family makes truly unique liqueurs and aperitifs at this winery, fondly known as "The Still on the Hill." All are single-barrel releases and are hand-distilled by a master of the art.

For the non-climbers, turn left for two flat blocks on Spring Mountain. A right turn and you'll be back on Madrona, four blocks from the starting point.

St. Helena has a wide range of dining opportunities; I only mention a few. Gillwoods is an easy place for meals that includes an in-house bakery. For world class dining with an Italian accent, try Tra Vigne.

WINERIES

Beringer Vineyards, 2000 Main Street, St. Helena 94574.
(707) 963-4812. Daily, 9:30–5:00; until 6:00 in summer.

Chateau Boswell, 3468 Silverado Trail, St. Helena 94574.
(707) 963-5472. Friday–Sunday, by appointment only.

Domaine Charbay Winery and Distillery, 4001 Spring Mountain Road, St. Helena 94574.
(707) 963-9327. Open by appointment only.

Rombauer Vineyards, 3522 Silverado Trail, St. Helena 94574.
(707) 963-5170. Daily, 10:00–5:00.

Spottswoode Winery, 1902 Madrona Avenue, St. Helena 94574.
(707) 963-0134. Open by appointment only.

STOPPING SITES

Gillwoods, 1313 Main Street (Highway 29), St. Helena.
(707) 963-1788. Open daily.

Tra Vigne, 1050 Charter Oak Avenue, St. Helena. (707) 963-4444.

Village Outlets of Napa Valley, 3111 N. St. Helena Highway (Highway 29), St. Helena. (707) 963-7282.

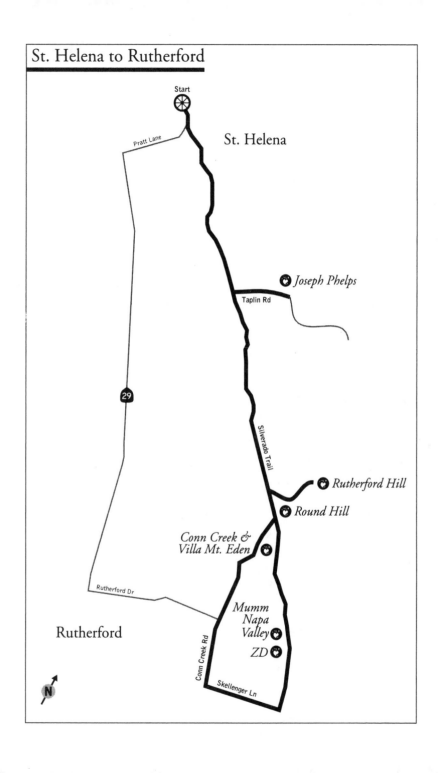

St. Helena to Rutherford

Start

Pratt Lane

St. Helena

Joseph Phelps

Taplin Rd

29

Silverado Trail

Rutherford Hill

Round Hill

Conn Creek &
Villa Mt. Eden

Rutherford Dr

Mumm
Napa
Valley

Rutherford

ZD

Conn Creek Rd

Skellenger Ln

N

⑱ St. Helena to Rutherford

Seven wineries, pretty ride with some hills if you like.

Approximately 17 miles

STARTING THE RIDE *This is classic Napa Valley riding with a couple of truly world class restaurants to tempt you. • Start at Pratt Avenue and the Silverado Trail, or hook up to it as an extension of the prior ride.*

Turn right heading south and enjoy the valley vista. In $4^1/2$ miles, you'll be at an intersection. Stay on the Silverado Trail and stop at the *Villa Mt. Eden at Conn Creek* tasting room, where two wineries with different agendas but common ownership offer complimentary tastings. Conn Creek uses strictly Napa Valley grapes that are sometimes blended into unique wines such as the Anthology and Meritage. The Villa Mt. Eden wines are blended with grapes from all over California for a wider range of tastes.

Continue your ride south, and in less than 1 mile *Mumm Napa Valley* will be on the right. This offspring of the famous French Champagne maker offers classic sparkling wine. Its tour is one of the best.

Turn right again, back on the Silverado Trail, and in less than $1/2$ mile *ZD Wines* will be on the right. This medium-sized winery produces twenty-five thousand cases a year. The de Leuze family operates this internationally renowned winery with only four non-family members on the staff. The aim here is to produce the most flavorful wines with the least amount of cellaring. This requires cool-climate grapes and skilled blending for depth. Chardonnay, Pinot Noir, and Cabernet Sauvignon are the signature wines.

Turn right and keep heading south. In a little more than $1/2$ mile, turn right at Skellenger Lane. Stay on this road as it makes a ninety-degree turn to head north. After the direction change, it is named Conn Creek Road. You're in delightful vineyards, so take a deep breath and enjoy!

After about 3 miles, you'll be back at the Silverado Trail and directly across from *Round Hill Winery.* Although their winery does not offer tasting, cyclists are welcome to fill up water bottles or purchase wine from the retail store. Revalee Hemken will offer you a warm welcome.

89

From the winery, turn right and head north; in less than $1/4$ mile you'll see the road that leads to *Rutherford Hill Winery*. The steady climb that leads to the winery is less than 1 mile in length. From the hilltop, the winery commands a great view. Frequent tours include a visit to its extensive caves, nearly a mile in length. Bill Jaeger and his family are the guiding force behind the winery. He was instrumental in the introduction of the Merlot grape to the Napa Valley, and Merlot is now the signature wine at Rutherford Hill. Seventy per cent of their hundred-thousand-case annual production is Merlot.

After your visit, check out Auberge de Soleil, to the left shortly after you leave the winery. The bar serves the fine food from the restaurant in an informal setting. The view from the deck is reputedly the best in all of the Napa Valley. The more formal restaurant is a bit upscale for sweaty bike folks. Make reservations to return for a really elegant meal when you're properly attired.

Cruise down the hill and turn right on the Silverado Trail. Ride north another $1^1/2$ miles and make a right turn on Taplin Road. It's $1/4$ mile to the entry gate of *Joseph Phelps*. The cattle grate is tricky; best to walk across this one. The steady climb to the winery takes you through some lush vineyards. In less than $1/2$ mile, you'll be at your destination. This winery offers formal tastings for a small fee and with prior arrangement only.

Head back and coast downhill. Don't forget about the cattle grate! Turn right and then right again when you reach the Silverado Trail. Make note of Howell Mountain Road, on your right, in $1^1/2$ miles; it leads to the Meadowood Resort and some excellent mealtime options.

Continue north and another $1^1/4$ miles will find you at Pratt Lane. Turn left and head back to St. Helena.

WINERIES

Joseph Phelps Vineyards, 200 Taplin Road, St. Helena 95474.
   (707) 963-2745. Open by appointment only. Tasting with tour only.
Mumm Napa Valley, 8445 Silverado Trail, Rutherford 94573.
   (707) 942-3434. Daily, 10:00–5:00.
Round Hill Winery, 1680 Silverado Trail, St. Helena 94574.
   (707) 963-5251. Tasting by appointment only. Water and shade always available.

Rutherford Hill Winery, 200 Rutherford Hill Road, Rutherford 94573. (707) 963-1871. Daily, 10:00–4:30.

Villa Mt. Eden at Conn Creek, 8711 Silverado Trail, St. Helena 94574. (707) 963-5133. Daily, 10:00–4:00.

ZD Wines, 8383 Silverado Trail, Napa 94558. (707) 963-5188. Daily, 10:00–4:30.

STOPPING SITES

Auberge de Soleil, 180 Rutherford Hill Road, Rutherford. (707) 963-1211. Reserve ahead.

Meadowood Resort Restaurant, 900 Meadowood Lane, St. Helena. (707) 963–3646. Reserve ahead.

Napa County

SOUTHERN NAPA VALLEY

⑲ Yountville, Stags Leap District

Eight wineries and a cute small town in a short ride suitable for a hot day.

Approximately 14 miles.

S TARTING THE RIDE *You can do this ride even if you didn't get an early start. Lots of good places to cool off along the way. • From Highway 29 or the Silverado Trail, turn off at Yountville Cross Road. State Lane is a small road that runs perpendicular to Yountville Cross Road about one mile from the Silverado Trail.*

Park anywhere on the shoulder of this tiny road near the driveway to *Goosecross Cellars,* which is about $1/2$ mile up the lane and on the left. Plan to visit after your ride; the cool winery makes a refreshing end to what can be a hot ride. Call first to make sure they'll be there to greet you. This small winery makes only Chardonnays and has an enviable reputation for high quality among the residents of the valley. Their wines are suitable for aging.

Head down State Lane and turn left on Yountville Cross Road. In $1/4$ mile *S. Anderson Vineyards* will be on the right. This is the smallest, and only single-family-owned, champagne producer in the valley. It uses a classic blend of Pinot Noir and Chardonnay for its premium champagne. With a production of ten thousand cases a year, you're not likely to find this at the grocery store.

Pedal another $1/4$ mile and make a right onto the Silverado Trail.

Since you only go south on this section of the Silverado Trail, wineries on both sides of the road are noted. There are enough in this short stretch that you can get a feel for the area without having to cross if traffic makes crossing difficult.

Robert Sinskey Vineyards will be on the left in about $1/4$ mile. The Carneros district supplies the grapes for its estate Pinot Noir and a proprietary Merlot. From the Stags Leap district, it produces a Cabernet-based Claret. The tasting room has a full kitchen, and food and wine pairings are sometimes offered, usually in the summer.

Turn left and continue down the trail. *Pine Ridge Winery* will be on the right in $1^1/2$ miles. Pine Ridge considers itself a Bordeaux-style winery with Cabernet Sauvignon as the flagship wine. The winery produces four estate-bottled Cabernets, each from a different designated vineyard.

93

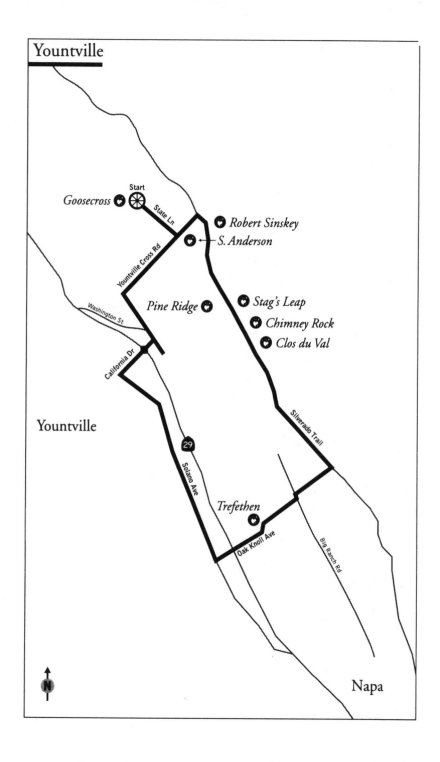

Yountville

Goosecross
Start
State Ln
Robert Sinskey
S. Anderson
Yountville Cross Rd
Washington St
Pine Ridge
Stag's Leap
Chimney Rock
Clos du Val
California Dr
Yountville
29
Silverado Trail
Solano Ave
Trefethen
Oak Knoll Ave
Big Ranch Rd
N
Napa

Turn right and continue your ride south. In $^3/_4$ mile, *Stag's Leap Wine Cellars* will be on the left. The Cabernet from this winery fooled the French experts at that famous tasting in 1976. It was mistaken for a fine Bordeaux! Mon Dieu! The Winiarskis are still in charge here, and they continue to produce wine that attracts connoisseurs from around the world to their unpretentious winery.

Turn left, back to the Silverado Trail. The stunning building that houses *Chimney Rock Winery* will be visible on the left in less than $^1/_2$ mile. With a production of fifteen thousand cases each year, this is a small winery. Bordeaux and Burgundy-style wines are made in the traditional French manner. Half of a golf course was bulldozed to create the winery and vineyards. Think of this as the ultimate nineteenth hole!

Back in the saddle, turn left and continue on your southerly path. In about $^1/_4$ mile, *Clos du Val* will be on the left. The traditional rose bushes greet you. The vineyard is on what long ago was a lava bed. This imparts a special quality to the grapes and the wine created from them. A full range of wines are produced here, from Cabernet Sauvignon to Chardonnay; tasting is complimentary.

Turn left and continue on the Silverado Trail. In almost $^1/_2$ mile, you'll see Chimney Rock Golf Course on the left. This is the half that didn't succumb to the bulldozer. Cafe Lucy at the golf course is open to the public. Lucy bakes all the bread and pastries herself. It's not your usual golf course fare, but then this is the Napa Valley!

If you're ready to hang up your wheels, the Painted Horses for sale down the trail about a mile might look tempting! Continue south to Oak Knoll Avenue, it's about $1^1/_4$ miles.

Turn right for a pleasant sojourn across the valley. In a little more than a mile, you'll run into Big Ranch Road. Oak Knoll makes a jog here; go left a few feet on Big Ranch Road, then right, back to Oak Knoll.

In $^1/_2$ mile *Trefethen Vineyards* will be on the right. This winery has six hundred acres of contiguous vineyards in the Napa Valley, the largest single block of ownership at the present time. Their estate wines include Cabernet Sauvignon, Chardonnay, and White Reisling.

Turn right leaving the winery and continue across the valley. In $^1/_2$ mile you'll be at Highway 29. What you want to do is cross the highway. How you want to accomplish this is carefully. A quiet road awaits you!

After you've crossed the highway, congratulate yourself! The railroad tracks that you cross carry the Wine Train. This is one of the newer, and more controversial, attractions of the Napa Valley. The train starts in Napa and serves a choice of meals paired with wines as it travels up and down the Valley. It might be a good alternative if you have nonbicyclists in your group.

Turn right onto Solano Avenue. The Red Hen will be on your left in about $1/2$ mile. This local attraction features an antique shop and a Mexican cantina and bar. Moderate prices and outdoor seating with a view make this a good choice.

Turn left after your visit, heading north. In $3^{1}/2$ miles you'll be at the intersection of California Drive. The Veteran's Home will be on your left. Turn right, passing under Highway 29.

Turn left onto Washington Street. You're in the charming little town of Yountville. Vintage 1870, a restaurant and shopping complex at the site of an old winery, is a short distance up Washington.

If you're ready for the direct route back, continue straight where Washington Street veers to the left. You'll be on Yount Street, which leads you back to Yountville Cross Road in about $1/2$ mile.

Turn right to cross the valley once more. In about $1^{1}/2$ miles, turn left on State Lane and finish your ride with a visit to *Goosecross Cellars.*

WINERIES

Chimney Rock Winery, 5350 Silverado Trail, Napa 94558.
   (707) 257-2641. Daily, 10:00–4:00.
Clos du Val, 5330 Silverado Trail, Napa 94558. (707) 252-6711.
   Daily, 10:00–5:00.
Goosecross Cellars, 1119 State Lane, Yountville 94599.
   (707) 944-1986. Open by appointment between 10:00 and 5:00.
Pine Ridge Winery, 5901 Silverado Trail, Napa 94558.
   (707) 253-7500. Daily, 11:00–5:00.
Robert Sinskey Vineyards, 6320 Silverado Trail, Napa 94558.
   (707) 944-9090. Daily, 10:00–4:30.
S. Anderson Vineyards, 1473 Yountville Cross Road, Yountville 94599.
   (707) 944-8642. Daily, 10:00–5:00.
Stag's Leap Wine Cellars, 5766 Silverado Trail, Napa 94558.
   (707) 944-2020. Daily, 10:00–4:30.

Trefethen Vineyards, 1160 Oak Knoll Avenue, Napa 94558.
(707) 255-7700. Daily, 10:00–4:30.

STOPPING SITES

Cafe Lucy, 5320 Silverado Trail, Napa 94558. (707) 255-0110.
   Daily, 7:00–6:30.

Napa Valley Wine Train, 1275 McKinstry Street, Napa 94559.
   (707) 253-2111.

Red Hen Cantina, 5091 St. Helena Highway, Napa. (707) 255-8125.
   Daily, 11:00–10:00.

Vintage 1870, 6525 Washington St., Yountville. (707) 944-2451.
   Daily, 10:00–5:30.

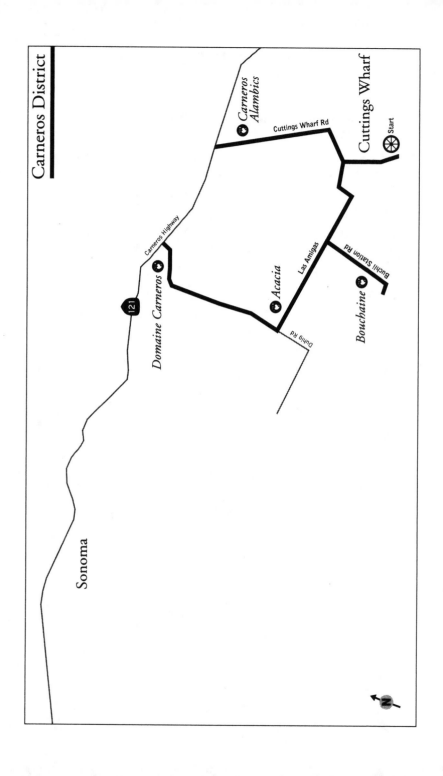

Carneros District

Sonoma

Domaine Carneros

Carneros Highway

Carneros Alambics

Cuttings Wharf Rd

Cuttings Wharf

Start

Acacia

Las Amigas

Buchli Station Rd

Bouchaine

Duhig Rd

The Carneros District

Rolling terrain that borders the Bay, three wineries and a distillery.

Approximately 14¹/₂ miles.

STARTING THE RIDE *From San Francisco head north on Highway 101. Turn off at the Napa/Sonoma exit. You will be on Highway 37. Turn left when you get to Highway 121; the signs guide you in the direction of Sonoma. Stay on Highway 121, also called the Carneros Highway in this section. Do not go into the town of Sonoma. Turn off at Cuttings Wharf Road. Drive to the end of Cuttings Wharf Road and park in the lot. Key Map B shows the major roads.*

The Carneros district has come into its own in the last twenty years. While I have grouped it with the Napa Valley, it is really an American Viticulture Area of its own. The Carneros district is in both Sonoma County and Napa County. Climate and growing conditions just don't respect our political boundaries. You can add this area on to the Sonoma Town Ride (pages 25–26). It is about ten miles from the town center, with some heavy traffic. If you continue on from the Napa Valley, I'd suggest a car for the approximately 15 miles from the Yountville Ride (pages 93–97).

You'll love the sleepy atmosphere here; not much traffic and lots of cows. The only time bicycles might be a problem is one weekend in April, when the area wineries stage a special event, April in Carneros, that draws many more cars than usual. Watch your dates when you plan to ride here.

Your departure point, Cuttings Wharf, was active from 1893 until 1909 as a shipping center for fruit destined for the canneries of San Francisco. Now it is a rustic fishing pier.

Start by riding ³/₄ mile to the intersection of Las Amigas Road. Turn left here, but watch that you stay on Las Amigas. It makes several sharp turns along its route.

The vineyards all around bear the names of many of the wineries that you have seen in the Napa and Sonoma areas. The Carneros grapes add a special flavor to the wine.

In about 1¹/₄ miles, turn left to Buchli Station Road. In ¹/₂ mile, *Bouchaine Vineyards* will be on the right. Started in 1980, this family-

99

run winery makes Pinot Noir, Chardonnay, Gewürztraminer, and Cabernet Franc. Complimentary tastings are by appointment and available every day but Sunday. You are welcome to picnic on the porch. Ride the $^1/_2$ mile to the end of the road to check it out.

Turn back and ride to Las Amigas and turn left. Continue along Las Amigas. You'll see cows lounging under the trees and simple country homes with chickens running around. This is a bit more authentic than the rarefied Napa Valley ambiance; abandoned houses and barns add to the reality.

In about a mile the *Acacia Winery* will be on the right. Again, an appointment is needed. Chardonnay is the principal wine here, with Pinot Noir a close second. These and the Brut sparkler are all made from Carneros grapes. Acacia's Zinfandel is made with grapes from the Howell Mountain area of the Napa Valley. Larry Brooks is the managing director and, more importantly, an avid cyclist.

Turn right leaving the winery and continue a short distance to the intersection of Duhig Road. Turn right here.

After $2^1/_4$ miles of nicely rolling hills, the impressive chateau that houses *Domaine Carneros* will be to your left. This winery is owned by the Taittinger family, famous for its French Champagne. The elegant building was inspired by the family home in France. The complete range of sparklers is offered in a stylish salon that has the feel of a fine restaurant. Tours are frequent and don't require advance reservations.

Return to Duhig Road and retrace the $2^1/_4$-mile ride on it to Las Amigas, where you turn left. Watch for the ninety-degree turns that are a characteristic of this road. In another $1^1/_2$ miles, you'll be at the intersection of Cuttings Wharf Road. Turn left.

In a mile, you'll see the entrance to *Carneros Alambics* on the right. This, the first alambic distillery in the United States, is owned by the Remy-Martin Cognac producers of France and was started in 1982. The first cognac was released in 1992. The brandy produced here is double distilled and carefully aged and doted on, much like a favorite child, for at least eight years. The distillery cannot offer tastings due to the high alcohol content, about thirty percent. A very informative tour, which includes a sniffing of various brandies, is available. This is a fitting last stop for the final ride of this volume.

Turn right as you leave and head back to the end of Cuttings Wharf Road.

The restaurant at the wharf, Moore's Landing, is open for three meals a day and is quite a local hangout.

If you've brought a picnic, eat on the dock overlooking the tranquil Napa River. You could be anywhere in the world; time stands still here. Savor the silence.

WINERIES

Acacia Winery, 2750 Las Amigas Road, Napa 94559. (707) 226-9991.
   Open by appointment between 9:00 and 4:30.
Bouchaine Vineyards, 1075 Buchli Station Road, Napa 94559.
   (707) 252-9065. Open by appointment daily, except Sunday.
Carneros Alambics, 1250 Cuttings Wharf Road, Napa 94559.
   (707) 253-9055. Daily, 10:30–4:30.
Domaine Carneros, 1240 Duhig Road, Napa 94559. (707) 257-0101.
   Daily, 10:30–4:30.

STOPPING SITES

Moore's Landing, 6 Cuttings Wharf Road, Napa.(707) 253-2439.
   Bar: daily, 10:00–2:00. Restaurant: weekdays,
   10:00–6:30 with a break between 2:00 and 4:00; weekends,
   7:00–6:30.

Index of Wineries

AND STOPPING SITES

A / B

Acacia Winery, 100, 101
Alderbrook Winery, 47
Alexander Valley Vineyards, 49, 51
Apple Farm, 72, 73
Arrowood Vineyards and Winery, 29
Arroyo Winery, 79, 82
Auberge de Soleil, 90, 91
Bartholomew Park Winery, 25, 26
Bellerose Vineyard, 45, 47
Belvedere Winery, 43, 44
Benziger Family Winery, 27, 29
Beringer Vineyards, 86, 87
Biscotti Notti, 72, 73
Blue Bird Cafe, 59
Boont Berry Farm Store, 72, 73
Boonville Hotel Restaurant, 72, 73
Bouchaine Vineyards, 99–100, 101
Brutocao Cellars, 72, 73
Buckley Lodge, 31, 32
Buena Vista Carneros, 26

C / D

Cafe Lucy, 95, 97
Calistoga Mineral Water Company, 79, 81, 83
Canyon Road Winery, 50, 51
Carneros Alambics, 100, 101
Chateau Boswell, 85, 87
Chateau de Baun, 41
Chateau Montelena, 79, 82
Chateau Souverain, 50–51
Chateau Souverain Cafe, 50–51
Chateau St. Jean, 31, 32
Chimney Rock Winery, 95, 96
Christine Woods Winery, 71

Clos du Val, 95, 96
Clos Pegase Winery, 81, 82
Conn Creek Winery, 89, 91
Cuvaison Winery, 82
Davis Bynum Winery, 44
De Loach Vineyards, 41
De Lorimier Winery, 50, 51
Dehlinger Winery, 39, 41
Domaine Carneros, 100, 101
Domaine Charbay Winery and Distillery, 86, 87
Domaine Saint Gregory, 57, 59
Dry Creek Vineyard, 45, 47
Dunnewood Vineyards and Winery, 61, 62
Dutch Henry Winery, 81-82

E / F / G

Ellie's Mutt Hut and Vegetarian Cafe, 62
Fellion's Delicatessen, 82, 83
Ferrari-Carano Winery, 53–54
Fetzer Vineyards, 57, 59
Field Stone Winery, 49, 51
Fisherman's Wharf, 18, 19
Floodgate Cafe, 71
Foppiano Vineyards, 43, 44
Fort Mason Center, 18–19
Fort Point, 19
Frey Vineyards, 63, 65
Gabrielli Winery, 63, 65
Geyser Peak Winery, 53, 54
Geysers, 79, 83
Gillwoods, 87
Glen Ellen Village Market, 27, 29
Goosecross Cellars, 93, 96

Greenwood Ridge Vineyards, 69, 71
Guaymas Restaurant, 18, 19
Gundlach-Bundschu Winery, 26

H / I / J / K
Handley Cellars, 69, 71
Hanna Winery, 49, 51
Hendy Woods State Park, 72, 73
Hop Kiln Winery, 44
Hopland Brewery and Restaurant, 59
Husch Vineyards, 71
Il Fornaio Panetteria, 18, 19
J. Fritz Winery, 53, 54
Jack London Village, 27, 29
Jepson Vineyards, 59
Jimtown Store, 49, 51
Johnson's Alexander Valley Wines,
    49, 51
Joseph Phelps Vineyards, 90
Joseph Swan Vineyards, 39, 41
Kendall-Jackson, 47
Kenwood Vineyards, 31, 32
Korbel Champagne Cellars, 37, 38
Kozlowski Farms, 37, 38

L / M / N / O
Lake Sonoma Winery, 53, 54
Lambert Bridge Winery, 45, 47
Landmark Vineyards, 31, 32
Larkmead Cellars Kornell, 81, 83
Lo Spuntino, 47
Mark West Estate Winery, 43, 44
Marketplace Shopping Center, 25, 26
Martinelli Vineyards, 39, 41
Martini and Prati Winery, 39, 41
Matanzas Creek Winery, 31, 32

Meadowood Resort Restaurant,
    90, 91
Meeker Vineyards, The, 54
Milano Winery, 57, 59
Moores' Flour Mill and Bakery, 62
Moore's Landing, 101
Morton's Warm Springs Park, 31, 32
Mumm Napa Valley, 89, 90
Murphy-Goode Estate Winery,
    50, 51
Napa Valley Ovens, 82, 83
Napa Valley Wine Train, 96, 97
Navarro Store, 69, 71
Navarro Vineyards, 69, 71
Obester Winery, 72, 73
One World Winery, 41

P / R
Parducci Wine Cellars, 61, 62
Pedroncelli Winery, 54
Pine Ridge Winery, 93, 96
Piper Sonoma, 43, 44
Porter Creek Vineyards, 44
Presidio of San Francisco, 19
Preston Winery, 54
Ravenswood Winery, 25, 26
Red Hen Cantina, 96, 97
Redwood Valley Cellars, 63, 65
Redwood Valley Vineyards, 63, 65
Robert Sinskey Vineyards, 93, 96
Robert Stemmler Vineyards, 45, 47
Rochioli Vineyard and Winery, 44
Rodney Strong Vineyards, 43, 44
Roederer Estate, 69, 71
Rombauer Vineyards, 85, 87
Round Hill Winery, 89, 90

Russian River Vineyards Restaurant, 37, 38
Rutherford Hill Winery, 90, 91

S / T
S. Anderson Vineyards, 93, 96
Sam's Anchor Cafe, 18, 19
Sausal Winery, 50, 51
Scharffenberger Cellars, 72–73
Sebastiani Vineyards, 25, 26, 27, 29
Silver Oak Cellars, 53, 54
Simi Winery, 49, 51
Smothers Brothers Winery, 32
Sonoma Cheese Factory, 25, 26
Sonoma County Farm Trails, 37, 38
Sonoma French Bakery, 25, 26
Sonoma State Historic Park, 27, 29
Spottswoode Winery, 85, 87
St. Francis Winery, 31–32
Stag's Leap Wine Cellars, 95, 96
Sterling Vineyards, 81, 83
Stonegate Winery, 81, 83
Sweden House Bakery, 18, 19
Sweets from the Heart, 47
Topolos at Russian River Vineyards, 37, 38
Tra Vigne, 87
Trefethen Vineyards, 95, 97
Trentadue Winery, 50, 51

V / W / Z
Valley of the Moon Winery, 29
Villa Mt. Eden at Conn Creek, 89, 91
Village Outlets of Napa Valley, 86, 87

Vintage 1870, 96, 97
Wellington Vineyards, 32
Whaler Vineyards, 57, 59
Windsor Vineyards Tiburon Wine Tasting Room, 18, 19
Z Moore Winery, 39, 41
ZD Wines, 89, 91

Notes